CHILDREN OF POVERTY

STUDIES ON THE EFFECTS
OF SINGLE PARENTHOOD,
THE FEMINIZATION OF POVERTY,
AND HOMELESSNESS

edited by
STUART BRUCHEY
ALLAN NEVINS PROFESSOR EMERITUS
COLUMBIA UNIVERSITY

PROMOTING LITERACY IN AT-RISK YOUTH

Protective Factors and Academic Achievements

SHARON L. QUERY
CHERYL O. HAUSAFUS

LONDON AND NEW YORK

First published 1998 by Garland Publishing, Inc.

Published 2020 by Routledge
2 Park Square, Milton Park, Abingdon, Oxon OX14 4RN
52 Vanderbilt Avenue, New York, NY 10017

First issued in paperback 2020

*Routledge is an imprint of the Taylor & Francis Group,
an informa business*

Copyright © 1998 Sharon L. Query and Cheryl O. Hausafus

All rights reserved. No part of this book may be reprinted or reproduced or utilised in any form or by any electronic, mechanical, or other means, now known or hereafter invented, including photocopying and recording, or in any information storage or retrieval system, without permission in writing from the publishers.

Notice:
Product or corporate names may be trademarks or registered trademarks, and are used only for identification and explanation without intent to infringe.

Library of Congress Cataloging-in-Publication Data

Query, Sharon L., 1954–
  Promoting literacy in at-risk youth : protective factors and academic achievements / Sharon L. Query and Cheryl O. Hausafus.
    p.   cm. — (Children of poverty)
  Includes bibliographical references and index.
  ISBN 0-8153-3226-2 (alk. paper)
    1. Poor children—Education (Elementary)—Iowa—Des Moines—Case studies. 2. Poor children—Iowa—Des Moines—Social conditions—Case studies. 3. Literacy programs—Iowa—Des Moines—Case studies. 4. Academic achievement—Iowa—Des Moines—Case studies. 5. Des Moines (Iowa)—Social conditions.
  I. Hausafus, Cheryl O., 1948–   . II. Title. III. Series.
LC4093.D47Q47 1998
372.18'26942—dc21
                                                        98-29806

ISBN 13: 978-1-138-98395-3 (pbk)
ISBN 13: 978-0-8153-3226-8 (hbk)

Contents

Tables and Figures	vii
Preface	ix
I. Introduction	3
II. Review of Related Literature	9
III. Method	31
IV. Results and Discussion	43
V. Implications	86
Appendix A: One-On-One Evaluation Form	88
Appendix B: Parent Survey	89
Appendix C: Teacher Survey	90
Appendix D: Journal Entry	91
References	92
Index	97

Tables and Figures

Table 1	Protective Factors at Each Level	30
Table 2	Description of Characteristics of Case Study Participants	37
Table 3	Sources of Evidence to Support Protective Factor Propositions	41
Table 4	Participants Ranked by Number of Protective Factor Examples	82
Table 5	Participants Ranked by Number of AcademicAchievement Examples	83
Figure 1	Model/CityWoodland Wilkie Literacy Project Interface for Selected Benson's Protective Factors within Bronfenbrenner's Ecological Model of Human Development	36

Preface

About one quarter of the children under the age of six are living in poverty, a factor that is highly relevant to school failure. It has been estimated that one quarter of the adolescent population is at risk of academic failure and other problem behaviors, with another quarter considered moderately at risk. School failure and the almost inevitable unemployment or underemployment that follows were among the most serious of these problems.

The media, politicians, program planners, and citizens often search for single factors and quick solutions to complex youth problems. The piecemeal approaches that result focus on a single risk factor to the exclusion of other known risk factors; these simplistic approaches have not and cannot be expected to work. Effective programs should address as many of these risk factors as possible. Researchers and practitioners have begun to look at protective factors which help shield students from school failure.

This book examines the relationship between protective factors and academic achievement in elementary students. Protective factors are individual or environmental safeguards that enhance a youngster's ability to resist stressful life events and promote resilience. There are protective factors at work in every system (individual, family, peer, school, and community.)

The authors studied participants involved in a project designed to increase protective factors and academic achievement. The results indicate that the participants exhibited an increase in academic achievement and protective factors. When considering the eight protective factors which were used in the original design of the project, evidence was found that those protective factors did occur: positive school environment, adult relationships, social skills, self-esteem, bonding to community, required helpfulness, problem solving, and a close friend. Study findings highlight the need to intentionally design youth programs which help to increase protective factors in young people, focus on providing young people the opportunity to bond with a supportive adult, and encourage the collection of qualitative data by volunteers and staff as they work with young people in their programs.

Promoting Literacy in
At-Risk Youth

CHAPTER I
Introduction

The Carnegie Council on Adolescent Development, in their publication *Turning Points* (1989), estimated that about one quarter of the adolescent population was at risk of academic failure and other problem behaviors, with another quarter considered moderately at risk. School failure and the almost inevitable unemployment or underemployment that follows were among the most serious of these problems.

Berlin and Sum (1988), in an insightful analysis of the effects of lack of basic educational skills on future opportunity, showed that those high school students in the bottom 20% of their classes were nine times more likely to drop out of school, eight times more likely to become parents out of wedlock, and four times more likely to go on welfare. Low school achievement and lack of basic skills always were included in analyses of the characteristics of high-risk youth, sometimes as antecedents or precursors, sometimes as consequences, and often as both.

The costs to society and to the individuals are high. Those who stay in school can avoid the risk of welfare: one added year of schooling means a 35% reduction in the chances of receiving welfare payments as an adult (Carnegie Council on Adolescent Development, 1989, p. 29). The nation pays the price not just in welfare payments, but in an estimated $26 billion in lost earnings and tax payments.

Only 28% of eighth graders in the United States scored at or above the proficiency level in reading in 1994. Two percent read at or above an advanced reading level. In 1990, 7% of the eighth-grade class of 1988 (most of who were then 15 and 16 years old) were dropouts. By their senior year (1992), 12% of this class were dropouts. Dropout rates varied by students' race/ethnicity: White (9.4); Black (14.5); Hispanic (18.3); Asian/Pacific Islanders (7.0); and American Indian (25.4) (Carnegie Council on Adolescent Development, 1996, p. 11).

The 1995 Iowa Kids Count data reflected the percentage of an age group that graduates from high school, on time, with their class. Iowa's rate was 86.7%; national figures generally present a graduation rate on this measure of 70-75% (Iowa Kids Count, 1995).

Most schools continued to sort students into *college prep, general,* and *vocational* tracks, with only the first group getting a curriculum that teaches critical reasoning and analysis. Poor and minority students still were the least likely to be placed in challenging courses. Nationally, about 65% of students from high-income families were placed in the college preparatory track, while less than 49% of students from middle-income families and less than 29% of students from poor families were placed in this track. Similarly, more than half of all White and Asian American students took a college prep curriculum, but the rate for Black students was 42% and for Latinos, 35% (Children's Defense Fund, 1996).

About a quarter of the children under the age of six are living in poverty, a factor that is highly relevant to school failure (Higgins & Mueller, 1988). Overall, an estimated 40% of children in the United States are at risk of school failure due to poverty, race, immigration, health problems, poor English language skills, living in a single parent family, or having parents with little education (National Commission on Children, 1991).

School failure is a real problem. As such, it has attracted the attention of researchers in psychology, sociology, and education. They have identified numerous factors that are associated with academic success or failure. These range from individual aspects of learning, such as behavioral problems and cognitive deficiencies, to family factors such as parenting techniques, to social issues such as poverty and cultural differences (Slavin, Karweit, & Wasik, 1994).

RISK FOCUSED, ECOLOGICAL APPROACH TO PREVENTION OF RISKY BEHAVIOR

The media, politicians, program planners, and citizens often search for single factors and quick solutions to complex youth problems

(Edelman, 1987). The piecemeal approaches that result focus on a single risk factor to the exclusion of other known risk factors; these simplistic approaches have not and cannot be expected to work. Effective programs should address as many of these risk and protective factors as possible. Researchers and practitioners have begun to look at protective factors which help shield students from school failure.

Hawkins, Catalano, and Miller (1992) contended that a risk focused approach in drug abuse prevention research was warranted given the apparent success of this approach in reducing risk factors for problems as divergent from drug abuse as heart and lung disease. The results suggested to Hawkins and his colleagues that perhaps a similar approach could be used for preventing problem behaviors in youth as well.

MODEL CITY/WOODLAND WILKIE LITERACY PROJECT

Des Moines, Iowa is home to 250,000 people. Easy for the general population to ignore, the symptoms of poverty (29.5% of the area's population) pervade on the near north side of the city. Almost 60% of children and youth in this area live in poverty. The infant mortality rate (36.7 deaths per 21,000 live births) in this area approaches that of third world countries. Adult illiteracy is estimated to be as high as 40%. Children watch drug deals go on in their neighborhoods, not just for marijuana, but for crack and methamphetamine. School personnel confiscate guns at middle schools, and other weapons from elementary students on a regular basis. In the 1994-95 school year there were 198 suspensions in the Des Moines school district for the possession and/or use of a weapon or other object that could be used to inflict harm or pain on another person (Des Moines Public School District, 1995). Drive-by-shootings and other gang-related incidents have become commonplace in the inner city of Des Moines. Minority ethnic and racial groups comprise a larger percentage of the population (55% White, 35% Black, 10% other minorities) of this area than other areas of the city and the state of Iowa.

The Model City/Woodland Wilkie Literacy Project began in 1991 and reached 507 five- to fourteen-year-olds yearly with long-term programming groups and intramural sports. The project was funded by the Cooperative Extension Service — United States Department of Agriculture as a national youth at risk site. The project provided comprehensive, intensive services to the target population and its overall goal was to increase school success so that youth can escape the cycle of poverty. The youth were involved in developing on-going, positive relationships with caring adults in informal educational settings. Collaboration among the agencies serving the population was enhanced through direct involvement in program delivery and community-based training programs. The project was designed to develop several protective factors: problem solving skills and intellectual abilities; self-esteem; self-efficacy and personal responsibility; social and interpersonal skills; close relationships with adults and peers; positive school experiences; required helpfulness; belonging to a supportive community; and bonding to family, school and other social institutions.

Some specific goals of the project were to:

- Help youth develop problem-solving skills, intellectual abilities, positive relationships with peers and adults, and positive school experiences.
- Assist parents, agency personnel and faculty to involve youth as resources in the family and classroom, empowering youth to impact their community.

Program assistants gathered detailed information about the participants with whom they worked and put the data in individual folios. The data were both qualitative (one-on-one observation forms, journals, and teacher and parent surveys) and quantitative (report cards). The data provided rich sources of evidence of protective factors and academic achievement for the individual participants. This method of gathering data, while time consuming for the program assistant, proved valuable in determining if protective factors were found and if academic achievement did occur for individual participants in the program. The folio method of gathering data should be of interest to other youth program professionals interested in collecting data on the prevention of youth problem behaviors.

PURPOSE

One purpose of the book was to determine if the participants in the Model City/Woodland Wilkie Literacy Project exhibited evidence of protective factors in their lives. A second purpose was to determine if participants in the Model City/Woodland Wilkie Literacy Project had increased their academic achievement.

Introduction 7

RESEARCH QUESTIONS

The research questions for the inquiry include:

I. Did the participants' folios exhibit evidence of protective factors?
II. Did the participants exhibit an increase in academic achievement?

DEFINITIONS

Pertinent terms used throughout the book were nominally defined to clarify their meaning. For purposes of this inquiry, relevant terms were defined as follows:

Adolescence: Adolescence is a period of life that is often mentioned as the time of transition between childhood and maturity (Newman & Newman, 1986).

Protective factors: Protective factors are individual or environmental safeguards that enhance a youngster's ability to resist stressful life events and promote adaptation and competence (Steinberg, 1989).

Risk factors: Risk factors are individual or environmental hazards that increase a youngster's vulnerability to negative development outcomes (Werner, 1990).

Literacy: The condition or quality of being able to read and write.

Folio: A compilation of detailed information about a participant collected by the program assistant.

CHAPTER II
Review of Related Literature

ECOLOGICAL MODEL OF HUMAN DEVELOPMENT

The clear message from the literature on child development is that human development is not greatly influenced by one factor, but rather by a whole mosaic of factors. Children grow up, not in isolation, but in ever-widening ecological environments. Children are influenced first and foremost by their family, but are also influenced by their peers, their school, and the community in which they live. Development has no single cause; rather multiple factors interact to shape development (Bogenschneider, 1996).

The ecological model of human development formalized by Bronfenbrenner (1979) was applied by researchers such as Benson (1990) and Bogenschneider (1996) to look at individual development as the result of a series of ongoing interactions and adaptations between the individual and a set of overlapping systems that relate both to the individual and to each other. According to Bronfenbrenner (1979): The ecology of human development involves the scientific study of the progressive, mutual accommodation between an active growing human being and the changing properties of the immediate settings in which the developing person lives, as this process is affected by relations between these settings, and by the larger contexts in which the settings are embedded. (p. 21)

It is Bronfenbrenner's emphasis in the *immediate settings* and the *larger contexts* in which the immediate settings and the developing person are embedded that is almost universally acknowledged as the cornerstone of the ecological frame of reference. Bronfenbrenner (1979) states: The environment, defined as relevant to developmental processes, is not limited to a single, immediate setting but is extended to incorporate interconnections between such settings, as well as to external influences emanating from the larger surroundings. This extended conception of the environment is considerably broader and more differentiated than that found in psychology in general and in developmental psychology in particular. The ecological environment is conceived topologically as a nested arrangement of concentric structures, each contained within the next. These structures are referred to as the micro-, meso-, exo-, and macrosystems. (p. 22)

A microsystem is a pattern of activities, roles, and interpersonal relations experienced by the developing person in a given setting with particular physical and material characteristics. A setting is a place where people can readily engage in face-to-face interaction — home, day care center, playground, and so on. The factors of activity, role, and interpersonal relationships constitute the elements, or building blocks, of the microsystem (Bronfenbrenner, 1979).

The microsystem is a set of relationships spinning out from a particular individual, and it also encompasses those relationships between and among the people in those settings. That means that the family becomes a microsystem, the school becomes a microsystem, the church becomes a microsystem, the peer group becomes a microsystem, and it becomes possible to categorize an organism's environment on the basis of the microsystems in which the individual participates (Garbarino, 1984).

A mesosystem comprises the interrelations among two or more settings in which the developing person actively participates (such as, for a child, the relations among home, school, and neighborhood peer group; for an adult, relations among family, work, and social life) (Bronfenbrenner, 1979, p.25). A mesosystem is thus a system of microsystems. It is formed or expanded whenever the developing person moves into a new setting.

Mesosystems are relationships between contexts or microsystems in which the developing person experiences reality. We measure the richness of mesosystems for the child by the number and quality of connections. The central principle here is that the stronger and more diverse the links between settings, the more powerful the resulting mesosystem will be as an influence on the child's development (Garbarino, 1992).

An exosystem refers to one or more settings that do not involve the developing person as an active participant, but in which events occur that affect, or are affected by, what happens in the setting containing the developing person (Bronfenbrenner, 1986a). Examples of an exosystem in the case of a young child might include the parents' place of work (for most children), a school class attended by an older sibling, the parents' group of friends, and those centers of power (such as school boards and planning commissions) that make decisions affecting the child's day-to-day life (Garbarino, 1992).

The macrosystem refers to consistencies, in the form and content of lower-order systems (micro-, meso-, and exo-) that exist or could exist, at the level of the subculture or the culture as a whole, along with any belief systems or ideology underlying such consistencies (Bronfenbrenner, 1979, p. 26). Within a given society, homes, day care centers, neighborhoods, work settings, and the relations between them are not the same for higher socio-economic families as for lower socio-economic families. The macrosystem is a blend of the institutional framework of the society and the ideology of the society, or to use a more evocative term, the *blueprints* of a society (Garbarino, 1984).

A recent advance in contemporary research on development in context has projected the factor of time along a new dimension. Traditionally in the study of human development, the passage of time was treated as synonymous with chronological age. Bronfenbrenner (1986b) referred to designs of this kind as chronosystems. Two types have been usefully distinguished: normative (entering school, puberty, entering the labor force, marriage) and non-normative (death or illness in the family, divorce, moving). Such transitions occur throughout the life span, and often serve as a direct impetus for developmental change. The term *life transition* refers to the developmental impact of a single event during a person's life.

RESEARCH ON RISK FACTORS AND PROTECTIVE FACTORS

The field of prevention, both in research and practice, came a long way in the 1980s: from short-term, even one-shot, individually-focused interventions in the school classroom to a growing awareness and beginning implementation of long-term, comprehensive, environmentally-focused interventions, expanding beyond the school to include the community (Benard, 1987). Furthermore, in the mid-1980s prevention practitioners began to discuss prevention strategies and programs based on research identifying the underlying risk factors for problems such as alcohol and other drug abuse, teen pregnancy, delinquency and gangs, and dropping out (Hawkins, Lishner, Catalano, & Howard, 1985). While certainly a major positive development, the identification of risks does not necessarily provide us with a clear sense of just what strategies we need to implement to reduce the risks. More recently, we have heard prevention practitioners talk about *protective factors*, about building *resiliency* in youth, about basing our strategies on what research has told us about the environmental factors that facilitate the development of youth who do not get involved in life-compromising situations (Benard, 1987). What clearly becomes the challenge into the 21st century is the implementation of prevention strategies that strengthen protective factors in our families, schools, and communities. As Gibbs and Bennett (1990) conceptualized the process, we must "turn the situation around by translating negative risk factors into positive action strategies" which are, in essence, protective factors (p. 20).

Historically, the social and behavioral sciences have followed a problem-focused approach to studying human and social development. This *pathology* model of research traditionally examined problems, disease, illness, maladaptation, incompetence, and deviance. This emphasis has been placed on identifying the risk factors of various disorders like alcoholism, schizophrenia and other mental illnesses, criminality, and delinquency. These studies have been retrospective in design; that is, they do a onetime historical assessment of adults with these existing identified problems, a research design that can only perpetuate a problem perspective and implicate an inevitability of negative outcomes. Furthermore, the data yielded from such research studies have ultimately been of only limited value to the prevention field, concerned as it is with building health-promoting, not health-compromising behaviors and with facilitating the development of social competence in children and youth. This pathology model of research has provided us with a false sense of security in erecting prevention models that are founded more on values than facts (Werner & Smith, 1982).

This retrospective research approach even became problematic for investigators focused on studying risks for the development of *problem behaviors* because they were stymied by the issue of whether abnormalities in people already diagnosed as schizophrenic, criminal, or alcoholic were the causes or consequences of schizophrenia or alcoholism (for example, is the lack of problem-solving skills usually found in adult alcoholics a cause or a result of drinking?). Consequently, with the exception of a couple of earlier studies, beginning in the late 1950s and on into the 1960s and 1970s, a few researchers decided to circumvent this dilemma by studying the individuals postulated to be at high risk for developing certain disorders — children growing up under conditions of great stress and adversity such as neonatal stress, poverty, neglect, abuse, physical handicaps, war, and of parental schizophrenia, depression, alcoholism and criminality. This risk research, therefore, used a prospective research design which is developmental and longitudinal, assessing children at various times during the course of their development in order to better understand the nature of the risk factors that can influence the development of a disorder (Benard, 1991).

As the children studied in these various longitudinal projects grew into adolescence and adulthood, a consistent and amazing finding emerged: While a certain percentage of these high-risk children developed various problems (a percentage higher than in the normal population) a greater percentage of the children became healthy, competent adults. For example, Bleuler (1984) found that only 9% of children of schizophrenic parents became schizophrenic, while 75% developed into healthy adults. He found remarkable evidence of strength, courage, and health in the midst of disaster and adversity.

Similarly, research by Rutter, Maughan, Mortimore, Ousten, and Smith (1979) on children growing up in poverty found that half of the children living under conditions of disadvantage do not repeat that pattern in their own adult lives. And, according to the often quoted statistic, while one out of four children of alcoholic parents developed alcohol problems, three out of four did not (Benard, 1991).

The above findings have resulted in a growing research interest in moving beyond the identification of risk factors for the development of a problem behavior to an examination of the protective factors, those traits, conditions, situations, and episodes, that appear to alter or even reverse predictions of negative outcome and enable individuals to circumvent life stressors (Garmezy, 1985).

Benson (1990), in *The Troubled Journey,* offered strong empirical data that provided evidence for validity of Bronfenbrenner's theory. His work was reinforced by ongoing work of Bogenschneider (1996) at the University of Wisconsin. *The Troubled Journey* reported findings of a systematic study of youth perspectives, values, and behaviors. Between 1989 and 1990, public schools in 111 communities in 25 states used Profiles of Student Life: Attitudes and Behaviors, a 152-item inventory developed by Search Institute. The report was based on the composite sample of over 46,000 6th to 12th grade students involved in these local studies. Benson defined 20 at-risk indicators covering nine categories or domains: alcohol, illicit drugs, tobacco, sexuality, depression/suicide, antisocial behavior, school, vehicle safety, and bulimia. Using the ecological approach, he then looked for evidence that internal and external assets (e.g., parental standards, positive school climate) and individual deficits (e.g., unsupervised time at home, stress, physical abuse, negative peer pressure) have an impact on at-risk behavior. Bogenschneider (1996) did a similar analysis using the concepts of protective and risk factors.

Between 1989 and 1995, Leffert, Benson, and Roehlkepartain (1997) verified the importance of the asset framework through studies of more than 250,000 sixth to twelfth grade youth in more than 450 communities nationwide. In 1996 Search Institute introduced an expanded framework of 40 assets for 12- to 18-year-old age group.

The core of the risk-focused prevention approach is quite simple. To prevent a problem from happening, identify the factors that increase the risk of that problem and then address those factors — either eliminate them or reduce their effects, or identify factors that protect against that problem and support or enhance those factors (Bogenschneider, 1996).

Risk factors are individual or environmental hazards that increase a youngster's vulnerability to negative development outcomes. The presence of a risk factor does not guarantee a negative developmental outcome, but rather, it increases the odds or probabilities that problem behaviors will occur (Werner, 1990).

Even in the case of overwhelming odds, some children exhibit a remarkable degree of resilience which leads to the question, "What is right with these children? What protects them?" (Werner, 1990, p. 97). Protective factors are individual or environmental safeguards that enhance a youngster's ability to resist stressful life events and promote adaptation and competence (Steinberg, 1989).

Protective factors are sometimes merely the opposite of risk factors; one major difference, however, is that risk factors may lead directly to disorder while protective factors operate only when a risk is present (Rutter, 1987). To reduce the incidence of problem behaviors among our youth requires addressing risk factors at multiple levels of the child's ecology. In one study by Rutter, et al. (1979), the presence of one risk factor (i.e., low social status) was not more likely to create dysfunction than when no risk factors were present; with two risk factors (i.e., low social status and severe marital discord), there was four times the chance of problem behaviors, and with four risk factors, the risk increased as much as 20 times.

Benson (1990) defined assets as factors promoting positive youth development. Some examples of assets are: experiencing a loving and supportive family; having parents who set standards for appropriate conduct; being motivated to do well in school; and caring about other people's feelings. The assets are at every level of the young person's environment: individual, family, school, peers, and community. The more assets an adolescent has, the lower the likelihood that there are at-risk behaviors. Sixth through eighth graders with only 0 to 10 assets had twice as many at-risk indicators as those with 11 to 20 assets, four times as many as those with 21 to 25 assets, and ten times as many at-risk indicators as those with 23 to 60 assets. Equally important, Benson (1990) reported preliminary evidence about the importance of having assets across the six asset types which include support, control, structured time use, educational commitment, positive values, and social competence. Using four key assets (positive school climate, family support, involvement in structured youth activities, and involvement in church or synagogue), Benson found that at-risk indicators are reduced almost on a one-to-one basis as key assets are added. Bogenschneider (1996) reached similar conclusions.

The importance of this research to the prevention field is obvious; if we can determine the personal and environmental sources of social competence and wellness, we can better plan prevention interventions focused on creating and enhancing the personal and environmental attributes that serve as the key to healthy development. The potential for prevention lies in increasing our knowledge and understanding of reasons why some children are not damaged by deprivation (Garmezy & Rutter, 1983).

PREVENTION PROGRAMS

Almost one-half of the youngsters in this country, aged 10-17, were estimated to engage in one or more of the following risky behaviors:

substance abuse, school failure, delinquency, or early, unprotected sexual intercourse (Dryfoos, 1990). Parents, policy makers, program directors, and the media have focused an enormous amount of attention on youth problems (suicide, teenage pregnancy, school failure, substance abuse, delinquency, and gangs) (Pittman, 1990). During the last 20 to 30 years, practitioners have experimented with a variety of different approaches to preventing problem behaviors in youth. There is a widespread view that "nothing works", that social programs are just "throwing money" at human problems (Schorr, 1988). Schorr, in her book, *Within Our Reach*, set out to examine and describe innovations thought to prevent or lessen damage to disadvantaged children and to consolidate the scattered evaluative information. The evidence Schorr amassed made a strong, credible case for the development of policies and programs for large-scale interventions on behalf of the poorest, most isolated children and their families. Investment in early education and children is particularly justified, she argued, in light of the long-term savings from the damage, which is prevented.

In an analysis of 100 model programs for substance abuse, delinquency, educational achievement, and pregnancy prevention, Dryfoos (1990) concluded that the successful programs share three common components: (1) almost all take place at school sites; (2) agencies or organizations outside the school carry the most responsibility; and (3) almost all incorporate more than one program component, relying on multi-agency, community-wide responses. Dryfoos cited the six components of successful prevention programs for adolescents to be individualized attention, early identification and intervention, social skills training, engagement of peers in interventions, involvement of parents, and a link to the world of work (Dryfoos, 1990).

McKnight (1993) discussed the importance of new partnerships being created by schools in the revitalization of community life. Three essential steps were outlined in moving the partnership concept from rhetoric to reality: (a) organize a group to explore how such a partnership might be forged in its community, (b) work together to create a vision of the ways in which this partnership could address key problems within both the school and the neighborhood it serves, and (c) try to get one or more mutually beneficial partnership activities up and running.

Dryfoos (1990) contended that high-risk children have many common characteristics: at early ages, they initiate a range of behaviors with negative consequences, they live in families with little supervision, they are often failing in school, they associate with children with similar patterns, and they live in high-risk communities. The issue for prevention programming, argues Dryfoos, is addressing these predictors of high-risk behaviors rather than the behaviors themselves.

For the clinician, intervention may be conceived as an attempt to shift the balance for the client from vulnerability to resilience, either by decreasing exposure to risk factors (such as the impact of parental alcoholism, poverty, or divorce), or by increasing the number of protective factors (communication and problem solving skills) (Werner, 1989b, p. 81). Protective factors are individual or environmental safeguards that enhance a youngster's ability to resist stressful life events and promote adaptation and competence (Steinberg, 1989). There are protective factors at work in every system (individual, family, peer, school, and community.) Each of these five levels was examined.

INDIVIDUAL LEVEL

The protective factors on the individual level include well-developed problem solving skills and intellectual abilities; sense of self-esteem, self-efficacy and personal responsibility; well-developed social and interpersonal skills; hobbies; involvement in a faith community; and achievement motivation. Each of these individual level protective factors was discussed.

Well-Developed Problem-Solving Skills and Intellectual Abilities

Cognitive factors such as a reflective rather than impulsive style of decision making and well-developed problem solving abilities were associated with reduced risk status. These cognitive abilities may have helped youngsters generate coping strategies for dealing with stress (Garmezy & Rutter, 1983).

Individual factors that can serve to protect children or youth from risk include well-developed problem solving skills and intellectual abilities. The resilient children in Werner and Smith's (1982) longitudinal study were not intellectually gifted, but they did possess well-developed problem-solving skills that they put to good use. For example, they seemed to be able to control their impulses and concentrate on their schoolwork even when their home lives were disordered and chaotic.

Sense of Self-Esteem, Self-Efficacy and Personal Responsibility

Correlational evidence suggested that it may be protective to have high self-esteem, a well established feeling of one's worth as a person, together with self-efficacy, a belief that one can have an impact on one's fate (Rutter, 1987). In contrast, a sense of helplessness increased the likelihood that one adversity will lead to another (Rutter, 1985).

Well-Developed Social and Interpersonal Skills

Resilient children seemed to have temperaments that elicited positive responses from other people (Werner, 1990), thereby increasing their capacity to attract and keep supportive relationships around them. This quality was especially important in eliciting competent parenting in early childhood, which set the pattern for later parent-child relationships (Werner, 1989a).

Resilient children tended to have temperamental characteristics that elicited positive responses from family members as well as strangers (Garmezy & Rutter, 1983; Rutter, 1978). They are often described as affectionate, active, cuddly, good natured, and easy to deal with. These same children had already met the world on their own terms by the time they were toddlers (Werner & Smith, 1982).

Several investigators have noted both a pronounced autonomy and a strong social orientation in resilient preschool children (Block, 1981; Murphy & Moriarty, 1976). They tended to play vigorously, sought out novel experiences, lacked fear, and were quite self-reliant. But they were able to ask for help from adults and peers when they needed it.

Hobbies

The resilient children on the island of Kauai, who were studied for nearly two decades, were not unusually talented, but they displayed a healthy androgyny in their interests and engaged in hobbies that were not narrowly sex-typed. Such activities, whether it was fishing, swimming, horseback riding, or hula dancing, gave them a reason to feel proud. Their hobbies, and their lively sense of humor, became a solace when things fell apart in their lives (Werner & Smith, 1982).

Involvement in a Faith Community

Involvement in a faith community protected children from involvement in drug abuse, delinquency, and teenage pregnancy. Regardless of the believer's religious affiliation or socioeconomic standing, faith appeared to give children and their caregivers a sense of coherence and stability, a belief that their lives had meaning, and the confidence that things would work out despite hard times. Religious belief could also teach compassion, allowing children to love despite hate (Werner, 1990).

Resilient children also seemed to have been imbued by their families with a sense of coherence (Antonovsky, 1979). They managed to believe that life made sense, that they had some control over their fate, and that a higher power helped those who help themselves (Murphy & Moriarty, 1976). This sense of meaning persisted among resilient children, even if they were uprooted by wars or scattered as refugees. It enabled them to maintain the ability to behave compassionately toward other people (Moskovitz, 1983).

Achievement Motivation

Research reviewed by Adams, Adams-Taylor, and Pittman (1989) strongly suggested that teenagers' decisions about sexual activity and use of contraceptives were tied closely to their perceptions of the opportunities open to them. Teenagers with strong achievement orientations and with clear goals for the future were less likely to become sexually active at early ages and more likely, if sexually active, to be regular and effective contraceptive users. In contrast, teenagers facing limited life options (limited resource teens and teens with low basic academic skills) were at greater risk of early parenthood (Adams, Adams-Taylor, & Pittman, 1989).

FAMILY LEVEL

Protective factors on the family level included a close relationship with at least one adult, family support/communication, structure and rules, parental monitoring, and school involvement. Each of these factors was examined.

Masten, Best, and Garmezy (1990) found that children who would otherwise be labeled *at risk* are unlikely to experience negative outcomes to the degree that one or more of the following was true for them:

1. They had a positive relationship with at least one competent adult or parent who was supportive.
2. They were good learners and problem solvers.
3. Their families taught them effective social skills so that they were engaging to others.
4. Their families helped them develop areas of competency valued by society and a strong sense of self-efficacy (p. 438).

Clark (1983) provided the findings of an outcome study in *Family Life and School Achievement: Why Poor Black Children Succeed or Fail*. He assigned to parents the critical role of influencing children's early learning experiences. This delegation to the child of responsibilities in home and at school accompanied by the transmission of family values provided for the acquisition of knowledge and the work patterns necessary for school achievement. A categorization of 17 patterns in the homes of high- and low-achieving children pointed out the differences rooted in family activities. For high achievers (low achievers are marked by direct opposites of these attributes), the following patterns were effective:

1. Frequent school contact was initiated by parent.
2. Child had some stimulating, supportive teachers.
3. Parents were psychologically and emotionally calm with child.
4. Students were psychologically and emotionally calm with parent.
5. Parents expected to play a major role in child's schooling.
6. Parents expected child to play major role in child's own schooling.
7. Parents expected child to get post-secondary training.
8. Parents had explicit achievement-centered rules and norms.
9. Students showed long-term acceptance of norms as legitimate.
10. Parents established clear, specific rule boundaries and status structures with parents as dominant authority.
11. Siblings interacted as organized subgroup.
12. Conflict between family members was infrequent.

13. Parents frequently engaged in deliberate achievement-training activities.
14. Parents frequently engaged in implicit achievement-training activities.
15. Parents exercised firm, consistent monitoring and rules enforcement.
16. Parents provided liberal nurturance and support.
17. Parents deferred to child's knowledge in intellectual matters (p. 200).

Close Relationship with at Least One Adult

Despite chronic poverty, family discord, or mental illness, most resilient children had the opportunity to establish a close bond with at least one caregiver from whom they received lots of attention during the first year of life (Anthony, 1974; Werner & Smith, 1982). Some of this caregiving came from substitutes within the family such as older siblings, grandparents, aunts, and uncles. Resilient children seemed to be especially adept at actively recruiting surrogate parents. The latter came from the ranks of baby-sitters, nannies, parents of friends or even a housemother in an orphanage (Moskovitz, 1983; Werner & Smith, 1982).

Resilient children had the opportunity to establish a close bond with at least one person who accepted them regardless of their temperament, attractiveness or intelligence (Werner, 1990). One good relationship did much to counteract the effects of other bad relationships (Rutter, 1985). A high-risk child needs to be attached to a responsible adult who pays attention to the child's specific needs.

Some studies also found this effect for relationships with adult non-relatives, such as a schoolteacher who took a special interest in a child (Werner, 1990). For others, emotional support came from a church group volunteer, a youth leader or favorite minister (Werner, 1990). When interviewed at 18, many resilient youths mentioned a favorite teacher who had become a role model, friend and confidant who was particularly supportive at times when their own family was beset by discord or threatened with dissolution (Werner, 1989b).

Family Support/Communication

Working with a sample of almost 1,000 eighth graders, Epstein (1983) examined the joint impact of family and classroom processes on change in student's attitudes and their academic achievement during the transition between the last year of middle school and the first year of high school. Children from homes or classrooms affording greater opportunity for communication and decision making not only exhibited greater independence after entering high school, but also received higher grades. Family processes were considerably more powerful in producing change than classroom procedures. School influences were nevertheless effective, especially for pupils from families who had not emphasized intergenerational communication in the home or the child's participation in decision-making. The effects of family and school processes were greater than effects attributable to socioeconomic status or race. Benson (1990) found families who provided high levels of love and support, and parents who were viewed as accessible resources for advice and support were assets for young people.

Parental Monitoring

Parental monitoring (Small & Eastman, 1991) involved a parent's supervision and awareness of a child's behavior and whereabouts. Although not as well documented in the research literature as other parental responsibilities, parental monitoring has recently been found to be an important factor in preventing adolescent problem behavior. Higher levels of effective parental monitoring have been found to be related to lower rates of sexual activity, drug and alcohol use, truancy, running away, and delinquency. Effective parental monitoring of adolescents does not mean that parents must always be present or that parents should be overly intrusive in their children's lives. Rather, it implies that parents show an active interest in the lives of their children and a willingness to enforce family rules and raise issues that concern them.

Data on adolescents' after-school experiences and their susceptibility to peer pressure (Steinberg, 1986) were derived from surveys administered to a heterogeneous sample of 865 adolescents in grades 5-9. Consistent with the findings of previous studies, Steinberg's results showed that adolescents who return to an unsupervised home after school are not significantly different from those who are supervised by their parents at home during after-school hours. However, when the sample of latchkey children was expanded to include greater variation in after-school experiences, adolescents who were more removed from adult supervision were found to be more susceptible to peer pressure to engage in antisocial activity. Adolescents who were home alone were less susceptible to peer pressure than those who were at a friend's house after school, and those who were at a friend's house, in turn, were less susceptible than were those who described themselves as "hanging out." Moreover, latchkey adolescents whose parents knew their whereabouts and those who had been raised authoritatively were less susceptible to peer influence than their peers were, even if their afternoons were spent in contexts in which adult supervision was lax and susceptibility to peer pressure was generally high.

Structure and Rules

Structure and rules in the household and assigned chores enabled many resilient children to cope well in spite of poverty and discrimination. This was true whether they lived on the rural island of Kauai or in the inner cities of the American Midwest, or in a London borough (Clark, 1983; Garmezy & Rutter, 1983; Rutter et al., 1979).

School Involvement

In a study of 10,000 high school students, Bogenschneider (1997) found that parents who were more involved in their adolescents' schooling had offspring who performed better in school. This was irrespective of the parents' gender or education and the children's gender, ethnicity, or family structure.

PEER LEVEL

The protective factors on the peer level included close friend and positive peer influences. Both of these factors were examined.

Close Friend

Resilient children found a great deal of emotional support outside of their immediate family. They tended to be well liked by their classmates and had at least one, and usually several, close friends and confidants (Garmezy & Rutter, 1983; Werner & Smith, 1982). In addition, they tended to rely on informal networks of neighbors, peers, and elders for counsel and advice in times of crisis and life transitions.

Resilient children were more likely to have one or more close friends than children who did not adapt as successfully (Werner, 1990). Resilient children also kept their friends for a long period of time and relied on them for emotional support. These friendships were most effective if they occurred in combination with a close and stable relationship with at least one family member (Werner, 1990).

Positive Peer Influences

Positive peer influence has been shown to be a protective factor. Students who associated with friends who model responsible behavior were less likely to exhibit negative behavior such as drug or alcohol use (Benson, 1990).

SCHOOL LEVEL

Protective factors on the school level included positive school experiences, favorite teacher, extracurricular activities, and educational aspiration. Each of these factors was discussed.

Positive School Experiences

Positive school experiences provided a source of strength amidst an otherwise chaotic environment. The benefits of a positive school experience can stem from academic pursuits but also from social success, a special relationship with a teacher, the opportunity to take positions of responsibility, or success in non-academic pursuits such as sports, music and art (Benson, 1990; Rutter, 1987). Children seemed most resilient in school environments that were warm, responsive, organized, and predictable with clearly and consistently defined rules, standards, and responsibilities; these characteristics appeared especially important for children experiencing transitions such as divorce. They seemed to have made their school a home away from home (Werner, 1990).

Research has shown that schools that establish high expectations for all students and give them the support necessary to live up to the expectations have high rates of academic success. Rutter found that schools in poverty-stricken areas of London showed considerable differences in rates of delinquency, behavioral disturbance, attendance, and academic attainment (even after controlling for family risk factors). The successful schools shared certain characteristics: an academic emphasis, teachers' clear expectations and regulations, a high level of student participation, and alternative resources such as library facilities, vocational work opportunities, art, music, and extracurricular activities (Rutter et al., 1979).

Resilient children were apt to like school and to do well in school, not exclusively in academics, but also in sports, drama, or music. Even if they were not unusually talented, they put whatever abilities they had to a good use. Often they saw school as a refuge from a disordered household (Wallerstein & Kelly, 1980).

In their studies of London schools, Rutter et al. (1979) found that good experiences in the classroom could mitigate the effects of considerable stress at home. Among the qualities that characterized the more successful schools were the setting of appropriately high standards, effective feedback by the teacher to the students, with ample use of praise, setting good models of behavior by teachers and giving students positions of trust and responsibility. Children who attended such schools developed few emotional or behavioral problems despite considerable deprivation and discord at home (Pines, 1984).

Favorite Teacher

A favorite teacher can become an important model of identification for a resilient child whose own home is beset by family conflict or dissolution (Wallerstein & Kelly, 1980). Early childhood programs and a favorite teacher can act as important buffers against adversity in the lives of resilient young children. Moskovitz (1983), in her follow-up study in adulthood of the childhood survivors of concentration camps, noted the pervasive influence of such a warm, caring teacher.

Extracurricular Activities

Participation in extracurricular activities or clubs can be another important informal source of support for resilient children. Many youngsters on Kauai were poor by material standards, but they participated in activities that allowed them to be a part of a cooperative enterprise, whether being a cheerleader or a member of a 4-H club. Some resilient older youth were members of the Big Brothers and Big Sisters Associations which enabled them to help other children less fortunate than themselves. For still others, emotional support came from a church group, a youth leader in the YMCA or YWCA, or from a favorite minister, priest, or rabbi (Werner & Smith, 1982).

Educational Aspiration

Students aspiring to pursue post-high school education were less likely to exhibit risky behavior (Benson, 1990). Data gathered from adolescents in a rural Wisconsin county found similar results (Small, Silverburg, & Kerns, 1992). Students were coded as either alcohol users or alcohol non-users, and as sexually active or not sexually active. In general, all students surveyed perceived benefits for alcohol use and sexual activity. The perceived costs that best differentiate sexually active teens from their non-sexually active peers included concerns about jeopardizing future educational or career plans, fear of getting a sexually transmitted disease, and a concern that either they or their partner might get pregnant. For both sexual activity and alcohol use, there were strong differences in the perceived costs between the two groups; both non-drinkers and non-sexually active adolescents perceived significantly more costs.

COMMUNITY LEVEL

The protective factors on the community level include required helpfulness; belonging to a supportive community; being viewed as resources; involvement in community organizations; and bonding to family, school, and other social institutions. Each of these factors was examined.

Required Helpfulness

In middle childhood and adolescence, resilient youth and adolescents were often engaged in acts of *required helpfulness* (Garmezy, 1985). On Kauai, many adolescents took care of their younger siblings. Some managed the household when a parent was ill or hospitalized; others worked part-time after school to support their family. Such acts of caring have also been noted by Anthony (1974) and Bleuler (1984) in their studies of the resilient offspring of psychotic parents, and by Moskovitz (1983) among the resilient orphans of concentration camps.

In addition, spending time on meaningful and important responsibilities may occupy the time and energy youth might otherwise devote to dangerous or illegal activities. The operational term here, however, is *meaningful responsibilities*. A number of studies have revealed that the positive effects of carrying out family responsibilities only becomes apparent to youngsters when their activities provide a real and necessary contribution to the family (Elder, 1974; Garmezy & Rutter, 1983).

Belonging to a Supportive Community

In contrast to youth with serious coping problems, resilient youth were able to rely on a greater number of sources of social support, including teachers, ministers, older friends, siblings and cousins, family day-care providers, nursery school teachers, neighbors, or contacts at social agencies (Werner, 1990). The beneficial effects of a supportive community appear to be strongest for children who are the most vulnerable (Steinberg, 1989).

The presence of social support benefited not only the child but also the parent. Regardless of culture and social class, a mother was warmer and more emotionally stable when there were more adults around to help. In fact, social isolation was one of the surest predictors of a child-abusing family; the mother's isolation was more closely related to risk, than to the absence of the father, according to Werner and Smith (1982).

The reclaiming environment is one that creates changes that meet the needs of both the young person and the society (Brendtro, Brokenleg, & Van Bockern, 1990). To reclaim is to recover and redeem, to restore value to something that has been devalued. Among the features of powerful *reclaiming* environments for youth are these:

1. Experiencing belonging in a supportive community, rather than being lost in a depersonalized bureaucracy.
2. Meeting one's needs for mastery, rather than enduring inflexible systems designed for the convenience of adults.
3. Involving youth in determining their own future, while recognizing society's need to control harmful behavior.
4. Expecting youth to be caregivers, not just helpless recipients overly dependent on the care of adults (pp. 2-3).

Viewed as Resources

The belief that young people should be viewed as resources in a community is based upon respect for the contribution young people can make to the planning, operation and evaluation of a youth-focused organization, family, or community. This belief acknowledges that any leadership and decision making roles involved can be shared by adults and young people. It is important for parents and children to be involved together in decisions which affect the whole family whenever possible. This may mean that both young people and adults need to learn the skills and attitudes necessary for shared decision making, and it may require some change in policy and administrative practice within the organization, or perhaps a reformulation of the organization's mission (Lofquist & Miller, 1989).

Involved in Community Organizations

Benson (1990) found that if students were involved in music, community organizations, or church or synagogue for one or more hours a week, they were less likely to display at-risk behavior. Participation in extracurricular activities — such as 4-H, the school band or a cheer leading squad, which allowed them to be part of a cooperative enterprise — was also an important source of emotional support for those children who succeeded against the odds. With the help of these support networks, the resilient children developed a sense of meaning in their lives and a belief that they could control their fate. Their experience in effectively coping with and mastering stressful life events built an attitude of hopefulness that contrasted starkly with the feelings of helplessness and futility that were expressed by their troubled peers (Werner, 1989a).

The kinds of community-based activities youngsters were engaged in and their exposure to the larger world also gave youth opportunities to develop skills and interests which, in turn, provided a foundation for future vocational and career choices. In addition, teachers, ministers, or other adults outside the family served as identification figures and sources of support when parents were absent or unable to do so. Finally, positive experiences with school or other institutions promoted youngsters' identification with the community and it's values, and may provide a sense of belonging and satisfaction with the larger world outside the family (Garmezy, 1983).

Bonding to Family, School, and Other Social Institutions

Attachment to parents, commitment to school and education, and an acceptance of the general norms and values of society inhibited both delinquency and drug use. Youngsters who felt emotional ties to their family, school or community were more apt to accept society-approved values and expectations for behavior, thereby increasing the likelihood that norm-changing strategies like *Just Say No* clubs, anti-drug media campaigns, and school policies about drinking would be effective (Hawkins et al., 1992).

In summary, the protective factors found in the literature review are listed in Table 1. The specific protective factors used to design the elementary grade level of the Model City/Woodland Wilkie Literacy Project are also indicated in Table 1. These specific protective factors were also selected for examination in this book.

Table 1: Protective Factors at Each Level

Level	Protective Factor
Individual	* Well-Developed Problem-Solving Skills and Intellectual Abilities
	* Sense of Self-Esteem, Self-Efficacy and Personal Responsibility
	* Well-Developed Social and Interpersonal Skills
	Hobbies
	Religious Commitment
	Achievement Motivation
Family	
	* Close Relationship with at Least One Person
	Family Support/Communication
	Parental Monitoring
	Structure and Rules
	School Involvement
Peer	
	* Close Friend
	Positive Peer Influences
School	
	* Positive School Experiences
	Favorite Teacher
	Extracurricular Activities
	Educational Aspiration
Community	
	* Required Helpfulness
	Belonging to a Supportive Community
	Involved in Community Organizations
	* Bonding to Family, School, and other Social Institutions

* Protective factors used in design of project

CHAPTER III
Method

The Carnegie Council on Adolescent Development in their publication *Turning Points* (1989) estimated that about one quarter of the adolescent population is at risk of academic failure and other problem behaviors, with another quarter considered moderately at risk. School failure and the almost inevitable unemployment or underemployment that follows are among the most serious of these problems.

The clear message from the literature is that children are influenced not only by their families but also by their peers, their school, and the community in which they live. Bronfenbrenner (1979, 1986b) has formalized the ecological model of human development. Much work has been done on determining protective factors that enhance a youngster's ability to resist stressful life events and promote adaptation and competence.

The Model City/Woodland Wilkie Literacy Project was designed to increase the participants' protective factors and their academic achievement. Some specific goals of the project were to:

Help youth develop problem-solving skills, intellectual abilities, positive relationships with peers and adults, and positive school experiences.

Assist parents, agency personnel and faculty to involve youth as resources in the family and classroom, empowering youth to impact their community.

CASE STUDY

The case study method was used to evaluate the impact of the Model City/Woodland Wilkie Literacy Project. This method was chosen because it required the collection of extensive data in order to produce an in-depth understanding of the entity being studied. Organizational case studies focus on an organization or a part of an organization such as the Model City/Woodland Wilkie Literacy Project. Case studies of this nature usually employ a variety of qualitative and quantitative methods over an extended period of time (Borg and Gall, 1989).

PURPOSE

One purpose of the book was to determine if the participants in the Model City/Woodland Wilkie Literacy Project exhibited evidence of protective factors in their lives. A second purpose of the book was to determine if participants in the Model City/Woodland Wilkie Literacy Project had increased their academic achievement. The book was limited to examining only the elementary grade level of the Model City/Woodland Wilkie Literacy Project.

RESEARCH QUESTIONS

The research questions for this investigation included:

I. Did the participants' folios exhibit evidence of protective factors?
II. Did the participants exhibit an increase in academic achievement?

PROPOSITIONS

Case studies outline propositions which will direct attention to something that should be examined within the scope of the investigation (Yin, 1984). The propositions were operationally defined to clarify their meaning. For purposes of this book, the propositions were defined as follows:

Positive Relationship with an Adult Participant has access to non-parent adult(s) for advice and support.

Positive School Experience School provides a caring, encouraging environment for participant.

Required Helpfulness Participants spend time on meaningful and important responsibilities such as caring for younger siblings or working part-time.

Bonding to School Participants feel an emotional tie to their school.

Bonding to Community Participants feel an emotional tie to their community.

Increased Academic Achievement in Reading Participants exhibit an increase in academic achievement in reading.

Increased Academic Achievement in Math Participants exhibit an increase in academic achievement in math.

Increased Academic Achievement in Science Participants exhibit an increase in academic achievement in science.

LITERACY PROJECT DESCRIPTION

The Model City/Woodland Wilkie Literacy Project used several strategies to accomplish its literacy goals. It focused on both elementary and middle school participants.

Project staff at four elementary schools conducted after-school programs, offered tutoring activities, and presented special interest activities. They worked one-on-one in weekly one-hour sessions with participants who were struggling academically. At any one time, the program assistants each worked with between 15 and 20 participants in the one-on-one sessions. Staff interacted with and observed the participants on the playground, in the lunchroom, and before and after school.

In the summer, elementary school age participants attended 240 contact hours at Extension- and community-staffed day camps that were designed to increase reading, writing, math and science literacy through learning centers, individual and group activities. Each summer up to 11 college students were involved in delivering programs to youth, experimenting with cutting-edge educational methods, such as class meetings, conflict resolution, and social skill development. The curriculum was developed by Iowa State University Extension and major partners, and was experientially based around the content areas of nutrition, science, communities, careers and art. Youth involved had significant input on specific activities. At least two hours were spent each day in reading, language arts, or math activities. At the end of each two-week session, youth planned and carried out a culminating activity involving their parents. The staff facilitated daily group meetings to involve participants in planning, group management, sharing, and group counseling.

Project staff facilitated insight groups, after school activities, field trips, job shadowing, and mentoring in two middle schools. The career education program involved small group sessions, field trips, job shadowing and a two-day trip to Iowa State University and the Iowa 4-H Environmental Education Center. Sixth grade bonding at the middle schools engaged youth in after school groups, small groups organized around student and faculty developed topics, and support groups. Volunteers at each school were recruited and trained for tutoring, mentoring and facilitating homework clubs depending on needs and available resources.

The parent education component developed skills and resources needed by parents to help their children. The program helped parents who had negative associations with schooling to become involved in their children's education through fun nights, parent education groups, student-run celebrations, and home visits. Parent education was facilitated in one-on-one or small group experiences for parents of both elementary and middle school participants. There were 26 agencies involved in providing meeting places, joint planning and training of staff, and there was commitment from building principals to assist in raising local funds for continuation of the Literacy Project.

Specific objectives of the elementary grade level of the project included:

Objective 1. Youth will maintain or improve their reading skills and begin to develop their curiosity and observation skills in order to see science and math as part of everyday life.

Objective 2. Youth will develop on-going positive relationships with peers and adults.

Objective 3. Youth will develop protective factors of: positive school experiences; required helpfulness; belonging to a supportive community; bonding to family, school and other social institutions.

Objective 4. Youth will learn and practice skills in problem solving, communication, and brainstorming to resolve conflict and manage their behavior.

Procedures for collecting data to support the Model City/Woodland Wilkie included:

- Individual folios on each participant who was involved in the project over a period of one summer or one semester. The participant's folio included samples of their own work; school attendance and grade records as available; one-to-one observation forms; and school activities data sheet.
- Personal observation—changes in attitude; demonstrated non-verbal behavior and skills as reported by staff, teachers, parents, and volunteers.
- Parent home survey—progress in school; participant's attitudes; and friendships.

Figure 1 depicts how the protective factors of the Model City/Woodland Wilkie Literacy Project interfaced with Bronfenbrenner's ecological model of human development. The shading on the figure represents the protective factors that were used in the design of the Literacy Project.

RESEARCH DESIGN

This inquiry used a single case, embedded design that examines one case or project and utilizes a variety of sources for evidence. The single case was limited to examine the elementary grade level of the Woodland Wilkie/Model City Literacy Project.

Sampling Method

A purposive sample was used. Nine participants were chosen who met all of the following criteria:

- had been in the program more than 18 months;
- had rich and varied data in their folio;
- had the same program assistant as their one-on-one tutor to help ensure consistency;
- had provided parental permission for data/records to be used in the evaluation; and
- together the sample group comprised a range of elementary grade levels and both genders.

Table 2 describes the participants selected for the study. The table indicates their gender, school, grade level, and calendar year(s) of involvement, activities, and types of evidence included in their folio. The participants' names have been changed to randomly selected initials to assure confidentiality.

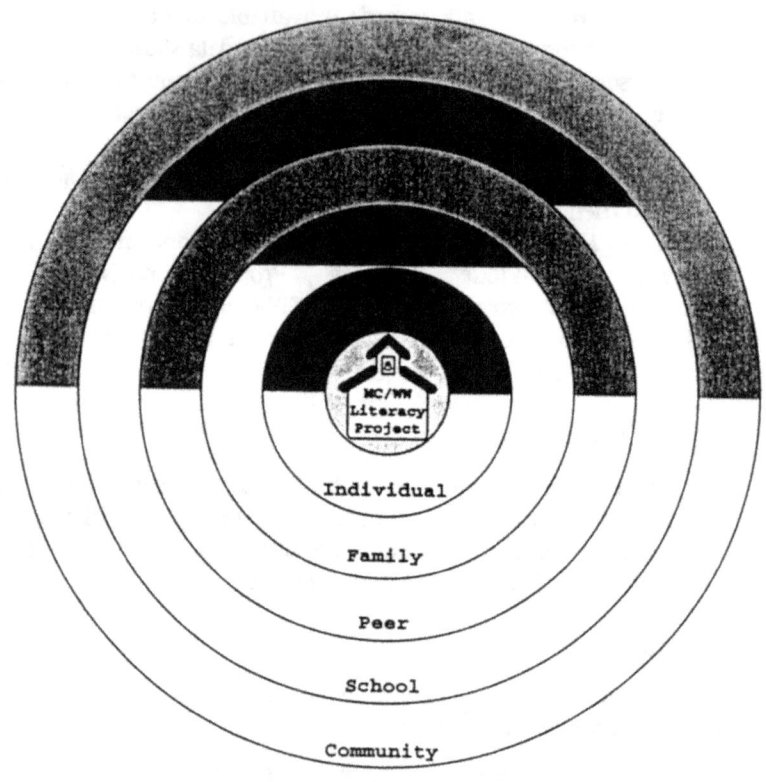

Figure 1.

Model City/Woodland Wilkie Literacy Project Interface for Selected Benson's Protective Factors within Bronfenbrenner's Ecological Model of Human Development. The shading represents the protective factors which are used in the design of the Literacy Project.

Method

Table 2: Description of Characteristics of Case Study Participants

Student	Gender	School	Grades	Years	Activity	Folio Evidence
L J	M	A	K-2	11/93-04/96	4-H after school	one-on-one grades activities parent teacher
R B	F	A	K-2	11/93-04/96		one-on-one grades activities parent
C T	F	B	1-3	11/93-03/96		one-on-one grades activities teacher
S W	M	B	2-5	10/92-03/96	day camp 4-H after school	one-on-one activities journal teacher grades

F L	M	B	1-3	10/93-03/96	day camp 4-H after school	one-on-one grades activities journal teacher parent
H M	M	B	3-5	10/93-10/95	4-H after school	one-on-one grades activities ITBS
W B	M	A	K-2	1/94-04/96	4-H after school	one-on-one activities grades
G Y	M	B	2-3	06/94-03/96	day camp	one-on-one grades journal activities
M D	F	A	1-2	09/94-04/96		one-on-one grades activities

The program assistant who worked with each of the participants was a white female, had a bachelor's degree in elementary education, and worked in the same two schools for over three years. She was trained in data collection for developing and maintaining the participants' folios. The training included involvement in the design of the one-on-one observation forms and in reporting functions. The program assistant received written and verbal feedback on a regular basis from the project director on the completeness of her data collection.

Data Sources

Evidence for case studies may come from six sources: documents, archival records, interviews, direct observation, participant-observation, and physical artifacts (Yin, 1984.) In addition to the attention given to these individual sources, three principles are important to any case study data collection effort. These include the use of: 1) multiple sources of evidence — evidence from two or more sources, but converging on the same set of facts or findings; 2) a case study data base — a formal assembly of evidence distinct from the final case study report; and 3) a chain of evidence — links between the questions asked, the data collected, and the conclusion drawn. The incorporation of these principles into a case study investigation will increase its quality substantially (Yin, 1984).

Procedures for Collecting Data

Data were collected by the program assistant working in the elementary schools throughout the duration of the project. Each elementary grade level participant had a folio that included a variety of material or evidence. This material included report cards, Iowa Test of Basic Skills (ITBS) scores, attendance records, school activities data sheets, parent surveys, teacher surveys, and one-on-one observation forms filled out by the program assistant. The one-on-one observation forms were filled out on a weekly basis, following each one-hour session with the participant. The report cards for the participants in grades K-2 indicated either N (Needs additional experiences) or S. (Steady progress). Participants in grades 3-5 were graded on an A-B-C-D-F system. ITBS scores were only gathered for one participant because ITBS were administered only to students in grade 3 and above, and one building principal did not allow the researcher access to the ITBS scores. Data in the folios represented data gathered from November 1992 to April 1996. Table 3 describes which evidence was used to gather information for each proposition.

Instruments

Examples of the pre-existing instruments used to gather evidence are located in Appendices A through D. They include a one-on-one evaluation form, parent survey, teacher survey, and journal entry. All forms were created by personnel for the Woodland Wilkie/Model City Literacy Project. The one-on-one observation form evolved over time, based on feedback from the program assistants and program director.

Validity of Research Study

Construct validity is the extent to which a study can be shown to measure a hypothetical construct (Borg & Gall, 1989, p.255). To meet the test of construct validity, an investigator must be sure to cover two steps:

1. select the specific types of changes that are to be studied (in relation to the original objectives of the study) and
2. demonstrate that the selected measures of these changes do indeed reflect the specific types of change that have been selected (Yin, 1984, p.37).

Three tactics are available to increase construct validity. The first is the use of multiple sources of evidence, in a manner encouraging convergent lines of inquiry. A second tactic is to establish a chain of evidence. The third strategy is to have the draft case study report reviewed by key informants.

Table 3: Sources of Evidence to Support Protective Factor Propositions

Propositions	Grades	ITBS Scores	Attendance	School Activities Data Sheet	Parent Survey	Teacher Survey	One-on-one Forms
I. Increased academic achievement in reading	X	X			X	X	X
II. Increased academic achievement in math	X	X			X	X	X
III. Increased academic achievement in science	X	X			X	X	X
IV. Positive relationship with peer					X	X	X
V. Positive relationship with an adult					X		X
VI. Positive school experience			X	X		X	X
VII. Required helpfulness							X
VIII. Bonding to School			X	X			X
IX. Bonding to Community							X

Treatment of Data

The data were analyzed using *Data Collector* (Turner & Handler, 1991), a computer program designed specifically for managing qualitative research. *Data Collector* enables the researcher to manage multiple evidence forms to analyze textual data obtained from interviews, observations, surveys, journals, and other documents in order to look for patterns and identify themes. The authors coded the data according to emerging themes. Possible themes considered prior to coding the data included reading ability, reading activity, reading motivation, math ability, math activity, math motivation, science ability, science activity, science motivation, relationship with program assistant, relationship with teacher, relationship with parent, relationship with friends, relationship with siblings, teachers showing an interest to student, bonding to school, and bonding to community. Although data were organized to answer the research questions: (Did the participants' folios exhibit evidence of protective factors? Did the participants exhibit an increase in academic achievement?) The authors also added new code words for themes that emerged during analysis. A one-third sample of data from each participant's folio was coded independently by two outside reviewers. Reviewer A had an 80% match with the researcher and Reviewer B had an 86.5% match with the authors. When the two reviewers' coding results were combined there was a 90.6% match with the authors for an interrater reliability of .91.

LIMITATIONS

This investigation was limited to describing the protective factors and academic achievement of elementary grade level participants in the Woodland Wilkie/Model City Literacy Project during the time period of November 1992 through April 1996. Although the elementary grade level phase of the project included two program assistants working in four schools, a limitation of the inquiry is that the data used here were gathered by one program assistant.

CHAPTER IV
Results and Discussion

The Model City/Woodland Wilkie Literacy Project was designed to develop protective factors in its target population. The purpose of this book was to determine if youth involved in the Model City/Woodland Wilkie project had developed protective factors which would in turn help them succeed in their school environment.

GENERAL DESCRIPTION OF PARTICIPANTS

There were nine participants selected in this case study. These participants were chosen because they met all of the following criteria:

- had been in the program more than 18 months;
- had rich and varied data in their folio;
- had the same program assistant as their one-on-one tutor to help ensure consistency;
- had provided parental permission for data/records to be used in the evaluation; and
- together the sample group comprised a range of elementary grade levels and both genders.

The program assistant who worked with each of the participants was a white female, had a bachelor's degree in elementary education, and worked in the same two schools for over three years. She was trained in data collection for developing and maintaining the participants' folios. The training included involvement in the design of the one-on-one observation forms and in reporting functions. The program assistant received written and verbal feedback on a regular basis from the project director on the completeness of her data collection. For the remainder of the book, she shall be called the assistant. The participants' names were changed to randomly selected initials to assure confidentiality. Initials were chosen instead of assumed names to help ensure that participant's identities were kept concealed. A brief description of each of these participants follows.

RB is a Hispanic female and was in the program from November 1993 to April 1996 while she was in kindergarten through second grade. She attended one-on-one tutoring. RB was referred to the program when she was in kindergarten. She didn't know her letters, numbers, or colors. The assistant focused on vocabulary, spelling, reading, social skills, playing together, problem solving, reading, and friendship skills in the one-on-ones. RB had many problems with speech and talking like a baby. RB talked a lot, so the assistant worked with RB on letting others have a chance to talk and share feelings. RB had an excellent relationship with the assistant. RB talked about the assistant often at home and would say hi to her in the hall. RB missed school often. She told the assistant that she got up late, or that Mom or Dad was tired. Her Mom seemed to believe that she had no part in RB's education.

WB is a black male and was in the program from January 1994 through April 1996 while he was in kindergarten through second grade. He was in after-school 4-H and one-on-one tutoring. WB's kindergarten teacher referred him to the program. He didn't know his letters, numbers, or colors. The assistant continued working with him in first and second grade on reading and math. His mother was not involved in any activities and would often sign the permission slips only after the children reminded her several times. WB started hanging around children that fight a lot. They were the ones that thought it was fun to be in trouble and wouldn't think twice when it came to fighting. WB was starting to show the signs that he could become like those children. WB always enjoyed working with the assistant. WB's self confidence in reading and math improved over the years. His relationship with the assistant had made him more comfortable to open up.

LJ is a black male and was in the program from November 1993 through April 1996 while he was in kindergarten through second grade. LJ participated in after-school 4-H and one-on-one tutoring. LJ had trouble with numbers, colors, and letters. Learning was difficult for him. When the assistant first worked with LJ, he was unresponsive. He didn't smile, didn't hug, and didn't answer any questions. As the

Results and Discussion

year went by, she saw LJ smiling, he gave her hugs, said hi to her in the halls, answered questions, and built higher-order thinking skills. He improved a great deal in his social skills. LJ improved in reading and self-confidence. He talked with more confidence. His reading was still low but he was willing to do all activities that his teachers asked of him. His reading lab teacher gave the assistant stories that LJ had read. LJ would argue with RB about who would read first. In kindergarten, LJ would say, "I can't do it." LJ's mother was picked up for shoplifting at several stores. The assistant smelled drugs on LJ's Dad's clothes. He didn't get to come to after-school 4-H the last year because he was going to Tiny-Tots day care. He was upset every week when he saw the assistant at another school and he couldn't come to 4-H. The assistant feared that LJ would slip through the system because he wouldn't be one that is well liked or is cute by other people's standards.

CT is a black female who was in the program from November 1993 to March 1996 while she was in the first through third grades. She was involved in one-on-one tutoring. CT was referred to the program by her first grade teacher because she needed help in reading. The assistant focused on self-esteem, sharing ideas, reading, and art in the one-on-one sessions. CT had a good relationship with the assistant. CT's mother sent the assistant a thank you card for doing all the nice things for her daughter. CT talked about 4-H with her family. CT had more self-confidence. She brought in a craft idea that she found at the library. The assistant and CT made a copy, read the directions and made it. CT's third grade teacher shared with the program assistant the writing assignments that the students had done. They had to write about their best friend and why they were special. Two of CT's classmates wrote about her. CT's mother has raised her alone and was involved in family fun nights. She knew what is right and wrong. CT didn't seem easily swayed when kids were doing "bad" things. She had good thinking and problem solving skills.

FL is a black male and was in the program from November 1993 to March 1996 while he was in the first through third grades. He attended day camp, after-school 4-H, and one-on-one tutoring. The assistant focused on talking softer, sight words, math, and following directions in the one-on-one sessions. His Dad took FL to camp and picked him up after school and participated in family fun nights. FL was a special needs student. He needed a lot of attention and didn't understand when he could not do certain things. He wanted to eat with the assistant at lunch. He read better and his math had improved.

MD is a white female and was in the program from September 1994 to April 1996 while she was in the first and second grades. She attended one-on-one tutoring. MD was referred to the program by a teacher who saw a problem with comprehension. The assistant focused on reading, following directions, listening, and reading with expression in the one-on-ones. MD had a good relationship with the assistant and often gave the assistant drawings and books she had made. The teachers talked to MD but were easily annoyed with her questions. MD moved to another state and her teacher was concerned, for she didn't think MD would adapt quickly to new things.

SW is a black male and was in the program from November 1992 to March 1996 while he was in the second through fifth grades. He attended summer day camp, after-school 4-H, and one-on-one tutoring. SW was always hesitant to try anything new. He would look at any activity the assistant had for him, and say he couldn't do it. The assistant tried to find art activities and games that he could find success at. His Mom was aware of 4-H. She often came in to pick up SW's sister and said how they both enjoyed 4-H and thanked the assistant for all the things she had done. He is very helpful and is very thoughtful of others. SW enjoyed working with the assistant. He didn't have a good relationship with his fourth grade teacher because "she was mean." His art teacher told the assistant that she could see great improvement in SW's self-esteem. She said he was willing to try things, he felt comfortable talking, and got involved more in class. SW was involved in Boys and Girls Club basketball. SW's parents were both involved in his life as his Dad coached his basketball team and his Mom knew what was happening in his life. He had friends who didn't believe in fighting, who enjoyed sports, and lived in his neighborhood.

HM is a white male who was in the program from November 1993 to November 1995 while he was in the third through the fifth grade. He was involved in after-school 4-H and one-on-one tutoring. HM was referred to the program because of behavior problems in the classroom. The assistant focused on social skills and problem solving skills during one-on-one sessions. His relationship with the assistant steadily improved over the time he was involved with the program, as did his social and problem solving skills.

Results and Discussion

GY is a white male and was in the program from June 1994 to March 1996 while he was in the second and third grades. He attended day camp and one-on-one tutoring. In school he often got into trouble; he threatened a lunch room assistant with a chair, got suspended from the bus for pulling the fire door alarm, and was often off-task. The assistant focused on adult relationships, behavior, and schoolwork in the one-on-one sessions. The only parent contact/involvement with the program occurred once or twice in the summer, when his parents were contacted about his behavior. GY had a friendly relationship with the assistant.

ANALYSIS OF EMERGING THEMES

All transcribed one-on-one observation forms were examined for themes related to protective factors and academic achievement. When reporting the transcribed folio notes, the authors made minimal use of editorial corrections of the assistant's recorded observations. When reporting, the following themes emerged from the data: increased academic skills (language, reading, science, spelling, writing, math, and problem solving skills); relationships with others (family, relationships with peers, and positive relationship with adult); personal characteristics (positive behavior, behavior problems, likes of the participant, and self concept); and process skills (bonding to community, following directions, required helpfulness, and social skills.)

Increased Academic Skills

The following themes were grouped under increased academic skills: increased language skills, increased reading skills, increased science skills, increased spelling skills, increased writing skills, increased math skills, and increased problem solving skills. A total of 185 examples were recorded by the assistant indicating increased academic achievement by the participants. These themes were consistent with the protective factors of well-developed problem solving skills and intellectual abilities found by Garmezy and Rutter (1983), Werner and Smith (1982), and Benson (1990).

Increased language skills

A total of four examples indicating increased language skills were found. These examples were all focused on helping the participant use proper English. The four examples follow:

> We played Garfield's "Go Fish." During this game, we work on proper English and asking for the particular card. "Do you have Don?" He is getting better at this. This helps because then he can associate the words on the card with the picture. Helps him read. He won the third game after two ties. He was really happy. Also on counting pairs — more and less. (LJ; One-on-one; 12/19/94)

> Worked on saying "have" instead of saying "got." (LJ; One-on-one; 3/13/95)

> Still working on saying "Do you have?" instead of "Do you got?" He has caught himself and corrected his question — progress! (LJ; One-on-one; 4/5/95)

> Played "Go Fish." Used proper English — Do you have? I didn't remind him once today. He caught himself three times. (LJ; One-on-one; 5/15/95)

Increased reading skills

A total of 88 examples were found of increased reading skills in the folios. The examples indicated increased skills in sounding out words, sight words, dictionary skills, phonics, alphabet, comprehension, and reading out loud. Each of the nine participants' folios included examples of increased reading skills. A representative group of 27 examples of increased reading skills follow:

> GY said he liked coming with me because it was quiet. The class is loud and says he can't get his work done. Had him read to me. He is a good reader. He sounds words out. (GY; One-on-one; 10/10/94)

We worked on word find/finish the sentence. GY said it was easy. We did another activity where he found a word using the first letter from each picture. GY is a good speller. (GY; One-on-one; 11/9/94)

We read a story. GY is a good reader. He is patient and tries to figure the word out. He reads like a storyteller. He changes his voice. (GY; One-on-one; 1/9/95)

Dictionary Skills — looking up words to find where the word originated. GY liked this. (GY; One-on-one; 12/19/95)

Worked on reading. She read the whole story. She tries really hard. She does do well at remembering the words I have written on cards. (CT; One-on-one; 11/23/93)

She really read this story well. We are adding words to her flash cards so she has a list of sight words she knows. I am going to send them home one day so her family can help her. (CT; One-on-one; 11/24/93)

I also started phonics with her. This is very difficult for her. She doesn't understand all the words end the same way. She had difficulties with sounds. (CT; One-on-one; 12/6/93)

We read today from one of my books. It was a difficult book but she did really well. I read some and then she would jump in and try. She read pretty well for the difficulty level. (CT; One-on-one; 12/15/93)

We worked on three pages on phonics. She has come a long way. When I first introduced her she could tell me all the sounds of the alphabet, now she can read the words knowing most of the words. (CT; One-on-one; 4/20/94)

Reviewed reading test. We went over several reading and language tests she missed a few on. CT did pretty well on them. The ones she missed she figured out the right answer. (CT; One-on-one; 10/24/94)

CT picked out "Some Fun" to read. She read the story smoothly. She only asked me two words. She has improved so much since first grade. She has also opened up a lot too. I saw her out at recess singing a song for jumping rope. Last year she would be just jumping. (CT; One-on-one; 11/7/94)

Read "Chicken Soup with Rice" — had rhyming in it and she read it smoothly. (CT; One-on-one; 4/19/95)

I read one page in "Freckle Juice." She volunteered to read the rest. Her reading has improved so much over the last year. More confident. (CT; One-on-one; 3/5/96)

Today I read a story that he picked out. He then went back and told his own story. Used good sound effects. (LJ; One-on-one; 4/13/94)

Knew the words red, it, Mom, Dad, is. He recognized those words without looking at the word. He found the word after just hearing it. (LJ; One-on-one; 4/12/95)

He did a nice job figuring out the covered up words in the story. Good comprehension of story — common sense. (LJ; One-on-one; 10/6/95)

Said he wanted to read to me. He went down to get two stories for him to read. He read wonderfully! He has come a long way. Still very hard on himself. Had a big smile when I clapped. (LJ; One-on-one; 3/8/96)

Did a super job matching beginning sound with pictures. She had no trouble at all. Worked well by herself too. She did really well at matching upper to lower case letters. (MD; One-on-one; 11/30/94)

Mrs. D said the MD read a whole page out of a story. She was shocked. It is really strange because she can't make sentences. She did really well on sight words. Will have to add more to her list. (MD; One-on-one; 12/14/94)

Mrs. D is amazed at what MD can read. Last time I gave her 11 new words and then went over them again and she could read them. (MD; One-on-one; 12/14/94)

Results and Discussion

He got really excited when I asked him to tell me all the letters he knew on the page. He knew most of them — hard ones were Q and all the vowels. (WB; One-on-one; 2/21/94)

He knows his letters and sounds. (WB; One-on-one; 4/17/95)

WB has improved some since last year. He knows his numbers and letters. We started working on blends — th, ch. He has a hard time. (WB; One-on-one; 5/22/95)

RB is improving this year. She knows all her letters and most of her sounds. (RB; One-on-one; 5/22/95)

Hooray! FL read his sentences, using his fingers to follow along. He didn't start making up his own sentence. I started off telling him what I expected from him and he did really well. (FL; One-on-one; 12/12/94)

He then read four stories from his folder. Today was a good day reading. He would make a mistake and read on. He then went back and corrected the error. I told him that makes a good reader. (FL; One-on-one; 2/23/95)

Mentioned that his teacher told him his reading has improved a lot. (SW; One-on-one; 4/25/95)

Increased science skills

There were four examples found in the participants' folios indicating an increase in science skills. These skills were focused on learning about the eye and conducting science experiments. Although developing curiosity and observation skills in science was an objective of the elementary grade level of the project, there were few examples of increased academic achievement in science.

Worksheet on the eye — he knew all the parts. (WB; One-on-one; 2/26/96)

He was really excited about learning about the eye. (FL; One-on-one; 2/25/95)

> Miss H had me work with him on his eye test. He knew most of the parts to the eye. He couldn't read his test but could tell me what everything was called. I was pleasantly surprised. (FL; One-on-one; 3/14/95)

> We started doing some science experiments. He got excited about a glider and asked to take it back to class and show them. (SW; One-on-one; 3/27/96)

Increased spelling skills

The participants' folios contained 13 examples indicating an increase in spelling skills. The examples included alphabetic order, orally spelling, and upper and lower case letters. Five participants had examples of increased spelling skills in their folio. To illustrate, six spelling skills examples follow:

> Had a worksheet on finding words in afternoon. It was lot of fun. GY found a lot of words and knew how to spell them. (GY; One-on-one; 10/24/94)

> Showed me her spelling test. She missed only one word. (CT; One-on-one; 1/12/94)

> We worked on spelling her words out loud. She did really well on all but two. Reviewed the two words again and she got them right. Smiled — happy with herself. (CT; One-on-one; 11/2/94)

> Wanted to do only 5 words in spelling, I asked her to spell all 10 and she only missed one — their. (MD; One-on-one; 5/17/95)

> Worked with upper/lower case letters. She only missed g,h,i,l,r. (RB; One-on-one; 1/4/96)

> Spelling — spelled all his words orally. (FL; One-on-one; 3/28/94)

Increased writing skills

There were 22 examples of increased writing skills found in the participants' folios. These examples included writing stories, cursive writing, writing complete sentences, and spacing between words.

Results and Discussion

Seven of the nine participants had examples of increased writing skills in their folios. A representative sample of ten writing skills examples follow:

> Says his Dad taught him cursive. He said, "My Dad sat me down with a stack of paper and we did the alphabet." Seemed happy that his Dad taught him. (GY; One-on-one; 10/31/95)

> Handwriting — his letters are small and he controls his hands better. His letters are recognizable now. (LJ; One-on-one; 3/2/94)

> LJ wrote his name on the top of the paper. I remember last year when I gave him a sheet and he couldn't even write his on the sheet. (Very large) His fine motor skills are improving — his letters are "normal size" and legible. (LJ; One-on-one; 12/12/94)

> His fine motor skills have greatly improved. He couldn't write his whole name LJ on a sheet of paper. Now he writes it on the line given. (LJ; One-on-one; 5/22/95)

> Journal — wrote three good sentences. I told her that was good, she wrote 2 more. Worked on what you need at the end of a sentence. I had to ask her 3 times. By the last sentence I looked at the sentence and then she put a period there. We finished coloring our names. She colored her background in just like mine. (MD; One-on-one; 3/13/95)

> Read and filled in the blanks. Does well when I don't watch her. When I do — she thinks she can't read. Told her what I wanted her to work on — spacing between words. She really focused on it and I could easily read her sentences. (MD; One-on-one; 5/8/95)

> Wrote a really nice sentence "S is for snow that falls down." She was concerned with spacing between sentences. She understands sentences. (RB; One-on-one; 12/12/94)

> Today we worked on handwriting. He did a nice job copying words. I even asked him to spell the words he just wrote. He got them all right. (FL; One-on-one; 4/20/94)

We worked on handwriting. He wrote much better. Miss H said it looked nice. (FL; One-on-one; 2/25/95)

SW is doing so well, his attitude is so much better. He's opening up more. I could see the progress in his journal. He's forming complete sentences now and has improved in his spelling, I'm so happy for him. (SW; One-on-one; 11/23/93)

Increased math skills

Examples of increased math skills were found 47 times in the participants' folios. The examples included counting, measurement, adding, subtracting, money, telling time, shapes, estimation, greater than, and less than. Seven of the nine participants had examples of increased math skills. To illustrate, 20 examples of increased math skills follow:

We also worked on counting. Doesn't have "counting on " skills like 1,2,3,4,5,6,7,8. (CT; One-on-one; 12/13/93)

I made up some math for her to do. She needs help with concept of adding and subtracting. She needs help counting up and backwards. I tried to make the problem relate to her. One was about her ponytails. She really got them a lot faster then "What's 1 + 1?" (CT; One-on-one; 2/2/94)

We worked on telling time. She has a hard time with little hand/ big hand. She did get better towards the end of all the practice. (CT; One-on-one; 1/11/95)

We worked on money today. It took her a while to tell me how much a penny, dime, quarter were worth. Then she counted pennies, dimes, nickels, really well, because she can count by one, five's, and ten's. She liked it when I gave her an example: You go to the store to buy candy for 15 cents. She showed me, then I asked can you think of a different way. She came up with 2 more ways. (CT; One-on-one; 1/18/95)

We worked on money again. We worked together and checked her math work. She still has a hard time telling quarters from nickels.

Results and Discussion

She can count by ten's and five's really well. She only missed one problem on her worksheet. (CT; One-on-one; 1/23/95)

Read and answered questions about populations in top four states. She answered the questions that were worded tricky, correctly. (CT; One-on-one; 4/17/95)

We worked on sorting shapes. He knows most of his shapes — rectangles are hard. (LJ; One-on-one; 12/15/93)

He could recognize 1, 2, and 3 without counting sometimes 4. (LJ; One-on-one; 2/9/94)

Dot-to-dot — did well with 1-8 but 9-12 didn't recognize. (LJ; One-on-one; 4/11/94)

Gave WB colored gummy sharks and had him separate out each color and count them. He did a good job counting. Then I asked questions for WB and RB. Who has more white sharks? How many green ones do you both have? (WB; One-on-one; 2/16/94)

He started to count his *Skittles* but he got mixed up, if he counted them. I asked, "How can you arrange them so that you know you counted them?" Confused. "Okay, when you were in kindergarten last year how did you move your counters to?" Didn't have to finish — he started to align them in a row and counted. Did a wonderful job. (WB; One-on-one; 3/29/95)

Had him group buttons into groups. First he put them into groups that look alike, 2nd by color, 3rd by size, counted the buttons. Then we used the buttons to make pictures. We counted how many petals, how many leaves, how many stems? This activity didn't seem to be hard for him. (WB; One-on-one; 4/12/95)

I asked him to show me 1 using two dice. He played with me and showed me one die with 1 on it. Then he said you couldn't make 1 with 2 dice. Then I asked him why I didn't go any higher than 12. "Because 6 + 6 is as far as you can go up." WB impressed me with his questions and thought. He has to count larger numbers (6+5=11).

He does know smaller numbers quicker (1+3=4). (WB; One-on-one; 10/9/95)

We also played "Go Fish" and she doesn't have any number recognition. She told me she couldn't count but once I started counting she got up to 20. (RB; One-on-one; 1/19/94)

Had her count her package of gummy sharks. They counted each color and found out who had more of each color. She did very well at greater than and less than. (RB; One-on-one; 2/16/94)

How many different colors in a pack of M&M's — graphs. We worked on counting graphing, adding. He didn't really understand all the work but he wanted to eat the M&M's. We got it done and he understood what color he had the most of. (FL; One-on-one; 5/17/94)

We worked on math. We grouped things into 5 and counted by five's. He did pretty good job counting by five's. He estimated pretty close to the actual amount in his container. (LJ; One-on-one; 3/1/95)

Word cards and math review. SW's attitude has improved so much, his confidence is building more and more. He is working with Mrs. B. She is his math/reading lab teacher. Our materials are consistent with hers in order to keep SW focused. I'm so proud of him. He says that he's studying his cards at home before he's allowed to play. He says he's doing this almost everyday. (SW; One-on-one; 11/9/92)

SW progressed well over the last few weeks working with the manipulations. I remember the first time we set them out he had great difficulty, and was very frustrated. But with consistent work he improved. SW completed almost all the chalk slate. On our first day he could only do two and that was pretty shaky. (SW; summer; 93)

SW did very well with the math wrap-ups. I thought that game would be helpful in improving his speed and accuracy. He really liked it so I told him he could take home one wrap up a week to practice. (SW; One-on-one; 12/7/92)

Results and Discussion

Increased problem solving skills

Seven examples of increased problem solving skills were found in the participants' folios. Cognitive factors such as well-developed problem solving skills may have helped youngsters generate coping strategies for dealing with stress (Garmezy & Rutter, 1983). Examples included working with opposites, logic, strategy, and what's wrong with this picture. Four of the nine participants had examples of increased problem solving skills in their folios. Six of the increased problem solving examples follow:

> I had a problem solving problem for him. He was to see how many triangles were in the picture. He counted all the obvious ones then I said can you see another triangle? Look at all the little triangles — they make a big triangle (which he counted). Can you see others inside those? He counted 7 more. We talked about not stopping after getting the "easy" ones — there are others. Fun. (GY; One-on-one; 2/20/95)

> We worked on opposites today. She did really well matching them. She even helped me come up with six more opposites I didn't have. She really likes to help out. She also always helps me clean up. (CT; One-on-one; 1/24/94)

> Logical thinking cards called "What's wrong with this picture?" RB is very good at logical thinking. She could tell me the wrong things so fast. She could even explain why they are wrong. Example: There was a sun with Santa going down the chimney. She told me that there wouldn't be a sun out when Santa is out. (RB; One-on-one; 2/29/95)

> Problem solving — played "Othello" game. (SW; One-on-one; 4/28/94)

> He wanted to play chess. He knows the rules pretty much but has trouble with plans and strategies. I try to talk through my strategies so he can hear why I moved the piece. (SW; One-on-one; 1/3/95)

Played "Pente" — a thinking game of strategy. He beat me twice. He is getting better at thinking ahead and planning. (SW; One-on-one; 1/3/95)

The above examples help to answer the second research question posed earlier Did the participants exhibit an increase in academic achievement? Statements of 185 examples of increased academic achievement were found in the participants' folios. Five of the participants each had over 20 examples of increased academic achievement, two participants had between 16 to 20 examples, one participant had 11 examples, and one participant had 3 examples. The examples of increased academic achievement ranged from:

- increased reading skills (88 examples),
- increased math skills (47 examples),
- increased writing skills (22 examples),
- increased spelling skills (13 examples),
- problem solving skills (7 examples),
- increased language (4 examples), and
- increased science skills (4 examples).

These results were consistent with the design of the program; the major focus of the literacy program was reading. Data also revealed that six of the nine participants had more examples of increased reading skills than any other area of academic achievement.

Relationships with Others

The following themes were grouped under relationships with others: family, peers, and ones only with an adult. Most resilient children have had the opportunity to establish a close bond with at least one caregiver (Anthony, 1974) or adult non-relative such as a schoolteacher who took a special interest in the child (Werner, 1990).

Family

There were 24 examples of family found in the participants' folios. The examples included the participant's relationships with their mother, father, siblings, grandmother, aunt, uncle, niece, and cousin. Most of the participants (8 out of 9) had examples of family in their folios. To illustrate, 11 examples of family follow:

Results and Discussion

Said he played "Sega Golf" with his Dad, brother and uncle all day on Sunday. We played, then had lunch then we played until I went to bed. (GY; One-on-one; 4/17/95)

Talked a little about his Grandma's funeral. Said it wasn't his first funeral. He said he didn't cry. He said it was scary the first time he went to a funeral. He seems to know and feel comfortable about death. He talked a lot about heaven. Was dressed up today. (GY; One-on-one; 5/1/95)

She told me she had one brother and then she said she had more brothers. She couldn't name them all. She also mentioned her cousin was living with her and had a dog. (CT; One-on-one; 10/27/93)

CT gets gifts from her aunt but I don't know how much her Mom does. She doesn't talk much about her Mom but a great deal of time talking about her aunt. (CT; One-on-one; 3/30/94)

Told me about visiting Grandma—she lives far away. (LJ; One-on-one; 11/7/94)

He wrote about his family, that he loved his Mom and Dad, and they went swimming together. (LJ; One-on-one; 3/29/96)

I asked him about his dad. He said his Dad moved but he knew where he lived. "He is living with his girlfriend." Do you like her? "Yes." That's good. (WB; One-on-one; 2/15/95)

RB talks about her sister a lot. They seem to get along most of the time. (RB; One-on-one; 10/24/94)

Easy to get along with. Very sweet. Loves to talk about her family and dancing. (RB; One-on-one; 5/22/95)

He started writing to his Mom today. He told me she lives in California. He told me he misses her. He wants his Mom and Dad to get back together. I told him that sometimes what we want can't happen. I told him about my Mom and Dad not being together. (FL; One-on-one; 11/24/93)

He said he had a "fabulous weekend." I asked, "What made it fabulous?" He said he got to spend time with his uncle. (FL; One-on-one; 1/23/95)

Relationships with peers

There were nine examples of relationships with peers found in the participant's folios. Examples included best friends, recess pals, and lunchroom friends. Five of the nine participants had examples of relationships with peers in their folio. Seven relationships with peers examples follow:

> K is his best friend. They goof off a lot in the lunchroom. (GY; One-on-one; 11/9/94)

> Gets along well with almost everyone. (CT; One-on-one; 3/8/95)

> His best friend is a girl in Mrs. C's class. (WB; One-on-one; 4/10/95)

> D is his best friend. (WB; One-on-one; 10/9/95)

> FL always says hi to everyone in the hall and often times they shake hands or high five. He seems to be liked by a lot of boys. (FL; One-on-one; 12/19/94)

> Got along with almost everyone. FL worked well with others. They seemed to treat him well. He played with the older kids. (FL; Summer Day camp; 8/14/95)

> SW says he plays football at another school with older kids. He says he likes playing with older kids. (SW; One-on-one; 10/25/94)

Positive relationship with adult

A total of 33 examples of positive relationships with adults were found in the participants' folios. All examples in the folios focused on the relationship of the assistant with the participants. Almost all of the participants (8 of 9) had examples of positive relationships with adults in their folios. A representative sample of 19 examples of positive relationships follows:

Results and Discussion

Very talkative today. He shared a lot with me about what he does. He talked about going to Special Art. He told me he got to go because he had super behavior. He was picked from his whole class. He made three beads and gets to put them on a necklace next time. (GY; One-on-one; 1/23/95)

Asked if he could come up for lunch. He brought J. (GY; One-on-one; 3/26/96)

I am very happily surprised at her comfort level in asking more questions. (CT; One-on-one; 3/28/94)

CT talks more than she did last year. I think she feels more comfortable with me. I am a familiar face. Still is quiet though. (CT; One-on-one; 10/24/94)

I know I say this a lot but CT has really opened up this year. She even came to me because a teacher sent her to get some paper from the next room. She wouldn't have asked me for help last year because she was always quiet. She says hi to me in the hall. Last year, I would start the conversation. Still a sweet innocent girl. (CT; One-on-one; 12/19/94)

Always stops in to talk to me before school. (HM; One-on-one; 1/31/95)

Wow. I had to make sure this was LJ. He was non-stop talk. He was telling me about his Mom & Dad, what he got for Christmas, that he can't play in the snow, . . . I was so surprised. It was really nice. He even smiled when I praised him for knowing all his colors. (LJ; One-on-one; 1/10/94)

He is opening up! Mrs. P mentioned this to me too. (LJ; One-on-one; 1/12/94)

Saw him at another school getting off the bus, he smiled, and waved at me. (LJ; One-on-one; 3/14//94)

Before class I was sitting in my room, and LJ came walking in. He walked right up and gave me big hug. Didn't say a word and left. He is not a hug-kind-of-kid, so it really surprises me when I get a hug from him. (LJ; One-on-one; 1/9/95)

LJ has changed so much. He is much more affectionate. He hugs me when I see him. He comes to talk to me before school. Last year it took me the longest time for him to smile. (LJ; One-on-one; 5/17/95)

Comes into my room several times a day — gives me a hug. (LJ; One-on-one; 2/26/96)

Came up to me in the cafeteria at breakfast and hugged me. Asked about me picking her up. (MD; One-on-one; 2/1/96)

We talked about moving some more. I told her I was going to miss her. She said, "I'm going to miss you. I'm not leaving yet." (MD; One-on-one; 4/12/96)

Invited me to her dance celebration. (RB; One-on-one; 5/22/95)

He came to visit me before one-on-one. Gave me a big hug. "Where have you been?" (FL; One-on-one; 1/10/94)

FL comes to visit me every morning I am here. He gives me a hug and shares something about himself (shirt, weekend, Mom, Dad.) He loves to talk. He is a helper at lunch and is doing a good job. (FL; One-on-one; 11/2/94)

Asked to come down for lunch. He likes to eat lunch with me. We talk a little. He gave me a God's Eye he made. (SW; One-on-one; 4/28/94)

Sometimes in my work, I reflect on if I'm making a difference. It is hard to say. But then I have to think of all the little things that I do for these kids. I am an adult they can say hi to in the hall — much more often after the 2nd year. I spend time individually, socializing. We talk and share a lot. We do work. I am a person who is their friend, even when they go to the next grade. I'm a stable person in their world of unstableness. With SW, I see that being there for him 2 years in a row, has helped him come out and share things I would never dream. I learned in a meeting that kids learn and care more if you care and have enthusiasm. (SW; One-on-one; 3/28/95)

The above examples of relationships with adults and peers help to answer the first research question posed earlier — Did the participants' folios exhibit protective factors? Statements of 66 examples of relationships with others were found in the participants' folios. The examples were of relationships with family, peers, or with the assistant. Examples of relationships with adults other than family or the assistant were not found in the data. This could indicate that there was a lack of other adults in the participants' lives, the assistant focused primarily on her relationship with the participants, or she had limited opportunity to discuss with them or observe other adults in their lives. Three participants had over 10 examples, two participants had 5 to 10 examples, and 4 participants had fewer than 4 examples of relationships with others.

Personal Characteristics

The following themes were grouped under personal characteristics: positive behavior, behavior problems, likes of the participant (including hobbies and activities), and self-concept. Werner and Smith (1982) found that resilient children had a healthy interest in a variety of hobbies and activities. Correlational evidence suggested that it may be protective to have high self-esteem, a well-established feeling of one's worth as a person (Rutter, 1987).

Positive behavior

Examples of positive behavior were found 29 times in the participants' folios. Examples included listening, taking turns, not talking back to an authority figure in the school, appropriate voice level, and focusing on the task at hand. Almost all of the participants (8 out of 9) had examples of positive behavior in their folios. To illustrate, 10 examples of positive behavior follow:

GY's behavior is very different when he is with me. Listens, doesn't talk back — knows and follows rules. (GY; One-on-one; 10/24/94)

GY does really well with me. His behavior is good. He is polite and takes his turn. It's hard to get him to say his behavior is ever bad in class. He denies everything. (GY; One-on-one; 1/11/95)

Mrs. H told me, in front of him, that he was having a good day. The stickers seem to work he has to get 8 out of 15 stickers for the day. He told me he is focusing on getting all 15 stickers for a day. (GY; One-on-one; 3/27/95)

Almost made two weeks without detention. (GY; One-on-one; 2/13/96)

Talked about his behavior sheet. He was really happy with his results. Doing well. Rewards—2 weeks of good behavior = lunch with Ms. E at McDonald's. (GY; One-on-one; 2/13/96)

Very quiet. Listens well. Very well behaved. (CT; One-on-one; 11/24/93)

HM said he is rewarded for good behavior from his teacher and from his Mom. (HM; One-on-one; 3/7/95)

Good behavior. Voice was lower and listened after first time reminded. (FL; One-on-one; 12/8/93)

They had sub in his class today. His behavior was really good. (FL; One-on-one; 1/19/94)

Good behavior. Focused more than usual. (FL; One-on-one; 1/26/94)

Behavior problems

A total of 26 examples of behavior problems were found in the participant's folios. Examples of problem behavior included lack of respect, talking in class, fighting, and threatening a staff member. A total of four of the participants had examples of behavior problems. To illustrate, six examples of behavior problems follow:

Results and Discussion

Miss H asked me to talk to GY about respecting the lunch/recess ladies. I talked to him and he explained that he was asked to go out in the hall but the other kid didn't. It all started when the kid took four pieces of candy of GY's and then GY took a piece back. It seemed to be that he was talking back because he wasn't being treated fairly. (GY; One-on-one; 1/4/95)

Not having problems with me but was suspended on Monday for threatening a recess assistant with a chair. (GY; One-on-one; 3/1/95)

Looked really sad — asked him why? "Didn't have a good morning." He said he was down in the office. I asked him if he changed his behavior after the office. "Yes." You will have bad times but the important thing is changing it. (GY; One-on-one; 5/1/95)

Ended up in the hall because he was talking. I stopped to talk to him and he didn't like it out there. "I can't get my work done." What do you need to do to stay in class? "Not talk." Okay, I'll check back to see if it works. (GY; One-on-one; 12/5/95)

It was exciting to hear HM tell me right off the bat that he was in detention yesterday. I asked him why & he said he had problems with the sub. Last time he was in detention it was because of a sub. I told him how proud I was that he told me about it. But that we had to work on this sub problem. He said he would and he knew that he tried to get away with more stuff when a sub was there. I told him next time there was a sub and if he made it all day I would take him on extra time that week. He was very excited and told me it was a definite deal. (HM; One-on-one; 11/13/93)

HM has trouble with his behavior when things don't go his way. If it doesn't work right away — he reacts. I talked with him about it. An example was when the new bus driver said she never heard of home drop-offs. So HM starts getting mad. "The bus driver, the black dude used to drive me home." Then he started mumbling under his breath. So I try to bring his behavior to his attention. I mention that if he didn't react so fast, or start treating people with disrespect that they would try to help you out. He at least heard, listened to me. (HM; One-on-one; 5/4/96)

Likes of the participant

Examples of likes of participants were found 54 times in the folios. These examples included playing outside, fishing, reading, dancing, basketball, art, checkers, 4-H, and football. Likes of the participant could also be classified as hobbies, which is a protective factor. All nine of the participants had likes exhibited in their folio. Thirteen examples of likes of the participant follow:

> He likes working with me. Very excited. (GY; One-on-one; 12/05/94)
>
> GY had fun making the bells. This surprised me. GY loves to wrestle, play outside, and be an outdoor kid. At the same time, he likes crafts and helping Mom bake cookies. (GY; One-on-one; 12/19/94)
>
> We talked about summer and fishing. He seems very interested in fish so I thought his next book would be about fish. (GY; One-on-one; 3/13/96)
>
> She really likes to help out. She also always helps me clean up. (CT; One-on-one; 1/24/94)
>
> Loves to make things — draw, color, and make crafts. (CT; One-on-one; 4/12/95)
>
> Likes to play soccer. (HM; One-on-one; 10/11/94)
>
> Very smiley today. LJ likes jokes and also is very curious when learning is made fun. (LJ; One-on-one; 5/16/94)
>
> He likes everything we do. He really likes sharing what he knows but not what he does. (WB; One-on-one; 3/2/94)
>
> We read "The Wheels on the Bus." He and I came up with some new verses. He likes to sing. (WB; One-on-one; 3/1/95)
>
> He asked me about summer 4-H. He likes to talk about 4-H. (FL; One-on-one; 2/9/94)

Results and Discussion

He gave me his artwork. He really likes to give me work he has done. (SW; One-on-one; 3/1/94)

SW says he plays football at school with older kids. He says he likes playing with older kids. (SW; One-on-one; 10/25/94)

Talked about his day off. Went sledding. Started basketball. Seems excited. (SW; One-on-one; 12/13/94)

Self-concept

There were 26 examples of positive self-concept found in the participants' folios. These examples included eye contact, confidence, posture, positive attitude, and self-affirmation. All nine participants had examples of positive self-concept in their folios. Examples of 18 positive self-concept entries follow:

Nice kid — feels good about himself. (GY; One-on-one; 10/10/94)

Better self concept — had a new outfit on. Read "Polar Bear." (CT; One-on-one; 2/14/94)

More eye contact. (CT; One-on-one; 3/9/94)

Good self-concept. Smiles a lot. (HM; One-on-one; 10/11/94)

He talked and had eye contact with me today. (LJ; One-on-one; 1/10/94)

LJ was very positive today. He did every activity with no comments. (LJ; One-on-one; 4/11/94)

Mrs. C thanked me for giving LJ success for the day. She said it is good for him to get one-on-one help and attention. (LJ; One-on-one; 1/18/95)

LJ has more confidence — shares what he knows. (LJ; One-on-one; 4/26/95)

The way he talks and carries himself makes me believe he is self-confident. He is willing to try new things. He feels safe with his teachers and with me. (LJ; One-on-one; 4/5/96)

It is hard to believe that this is the same kid I worked with in kindergarten. He smiles, shows his feelings, he hugs me, talks, shares what he thinks, and he "fights" for what he thinks is right. When I worked with LJ in kindergarten, he was not self-confident, didn't try, didn't smile, and was very hard to talk to. (LJ; One-on-one; 4/12/95)

More confident and independent today. (MD; One-on-one; 4/19/95)

Did her work without me saying everything was okay. Didn't have to ask, "Do I do a good job?" (MD; One-on-one; 4/24/95)

She said, "I am smart. I am a (last name)." (RB; One-on-one; 5/4/94)

Good self-concept. (RB; One-on-one; 9/26/94)

She seems more confident in herself. (RB; One-on-one; 3/29/96

Good self-concept. (FL; One-on-one; 11/1/93)

SW really liked the worksheet. He liked finding what was wrong in the picture. SW has more confidence. He is trying things. Last year I felt bad because I couldn't get him to try anything new. If I start with something easy, he hooks right into the task. (SW; One-on-one; 10/20/94)

Mrs. G stopped me in the hall and told me the teachers were talking about how happy SW is this year. She said it is all my doing. I said I think his confidence level is high because he sees success in the self-contained classroom. (SW; One-on-one; 3/7/95)

The above examples of positive behavior, likes of participants, and self-concept help to answer the second research question posed earlier, "Did the participants' folios exhibit protective factors?" In all, 109 examples of the protective factors of positive behavior, likes of the

Results and Discussion

participant, and self-concept were found with the participants' folios. Two participants each had over 20 examples, four participants each had 10 to 20 examples, and three participants each had 5 to 9 examples.

Process Skills

The following themes were grouped under process skills: bonding to community, following directions, required helpfulness, and social skills. Attachment to and participation in community based activities such as basketball and after-school 4-H inhibited at-risk behavior (Benson, 1990). In middle childhood, resilient youth were often engaged in acts of required helpfulness (Garmezy, 1985). Resilient children seemed to have temperaments and display social skills that elicited positive responses from other people (Werner, 1990).

Bonding to community

Examples of bonding to community were found 18 times in the participants' folios. Examples of bonding to community included after-school 4-H, basketball, and Boys and Girls Club. Seven of the nine participants had bonding to community exhibited in their folios. To illustrate, 11 examples of bonding to community follow:

> CT may be able to come to summer camp, I think this would help her develop in reading. (CT; One-on-one; 4/20/94)

> Invited me to his basketball game on Saturday at the Wilkie House. He says, he is the best. (HM; One-on-one; 3/9/95)

> Played basketball at recess — talked about soccer. Plays for Model Cities team. (HM; One-on-one; 4/25/95)

> Excited that he is coming to after-school 4-H next week. (LJ; One-on-one; 11/2/94)

> Loves after-school 4-H. (RB; One-on-one; 9/26/94)

> FL was at the Special Olympics on Monday. He said he got second place. "I almost got the trophy." (FL; One-on-one; 4/27/94)

I wanted to talk to the kids about fundraising and just mentioned it at after-school 4-H. FL remembered the next day and said I think we should make more cards to make them feel good. And make pictures. I was so proud that he was listening. I praised him for it. (FL; One-on-one; 3/6/95)

Didn't work with SW today because he was in an assembly. Mrs. T told me he was staying after for awhile. He straightened up after that. He loves 4-H so much that this motivates him to do his work. She really enjoys working with him — "He's so cute." (SW; One-on-one; 12/7/93)

When I went to pick up SW this girl came over and asked if she could come. I told her that I just work with SW and that the teachers tell me who to work with. SW told me he talked to her about 4-H all the time. This is probably why she wanted to come with us. (SW; One-on-one; 12/16/93)

He told me about his basketball games. His Dad coaches the team. They practice at Model Cities and Homes of Oakridge. (SW; One-on-one; 2/24/94)

SW is easier to talk to this year. He came to after-school 4-H today. He interacted well today. (SW; One-on-one; 11/29/94)

Following directions

There were 23 examples of following directions in the participants' folios. A total of six of the participants had examples of following directions in their folios. A sample of eight examples of following directions follows:

Did a super job at following directions today. I had him locating letters that I would say. He found every letter I said. (LJ; One-on-one; 12/12/94)

I helped her with her journal, she wrote a complete sentence and I rewarded her for it. Then I tried to get her to finish two other sentences she didn't finish. She did a super job following directions on this. (MD; One-on-one; 12/12/94)

Results and Discussion

We made decorations for his teacher. He did a good job following directions. (FL; One-on-one; 12/14/94)

Mrs. P was gone today because her father was in the hospital. FL told me this. We made clapper bells with glitter to them. He had three—one for his teacher, one for Mrs. E, and one for his tree at home. He really loved all the glitter. He did a super job at listening and following directions. (FL; One-on-one; 12/19/94)

He tried to teach me a 6-point star again. He forgot the 3rd step, so I taught him how to make a paper balloon. He did a great job at following directions and staying with me. He liked making one for himself. (SW; One-on-one; 12/2/93)

Finished making the flower. Said it was hard. He listened very well by doing what I told him — followed directions. (GY; One-on-one; 4/17/95)

RB and WB are very good listeners. We read the story Ten in the Bed. Today RB did a super job taking turns, sometimes she gets excited and tells the answer. (RB; One-on-one; 4/27/94)

Followed directions and colored really well—good hand coordination. Had a worksheet on objects that go together. I asked her why the objects go together. She explained them beautifully. She still talks at times like a baby. (RB; One-on-one; 11/21/94)

Required helpfulness

There were 16 examples of required helpfulness in the participants' folios. Examples include cleaning up, setting up chairs, returning a lost library card, and helping with a bulletin board. Examples of required helpfulness were found in seven of the nine participants' folios. To illustrate, 13 examples of required helpfulness follow:

She is always picking up the games and pieces when we are ready to go. (CT; One-on-one; 2/9/94)

She helped LJ with some of the numbers. I think this made her feel good. (CT; One-on-one; 4/13/94)

Held the trash can lid for me—very thoughtful. Helped clean up without any one saying anything. (CT; One-on-one; 1/30/96)

Told me his Mom gave him candy for helping at home. (LJ; One-on-one; 3/28/94)

Did really well in 4-H. Didn't complain that he couldn't do something. Helped me pass out several things. (LJ; One-on-one; 3/13/95)

She said she wanted me to write to her. She said she is going to be a helper when she moves. (MD; One-on-one; 4/22/96)

Very helpful. (WB; One-on-one; 4/10/95)

Helped me decorate the bulletin board by drawing and writing about his favorite books, "Clifford, the Dog." (WB; One-on-one; 11/27/95)

In 4-H after-school she realized we had to clean up before we played. (WB; One-on-one; 12/11/95)

At 4-H, F came in for her class. I told F that I could help her after 4-H. WB said he would like to help too. We all helped F move chairs into the gym. WB is a very giving person. (WB; One-on-one; 3/25/96)

FL found a library card in the hall and wanted to return it to the owner. So we took a walk down to Room 103. I wanted him to be understood so I went over how you talk to someone. He did a good job and was well understood. (FL; One-on-one; 2/16/94)

Helped out. Said, "This is fun, helping out a teacher." (SW; One-on-one; 10/13/94)

Helped me come up with a title for our bulletin board. He thought up, "4-H with L and the Best Kids." I thought it was great. (SW; One-on-one; 3/28/95)

Results and Discussion

Social skills

There were 32 examples of social skills found in the participants' folios. Examples of social skills include saying thank you, giving compliments, honesty, manners, and controlling their temper. Almost all of the participants (8 out of 9) had examples of social skills in their folios. A sample of 20 examples of social skills follows:

> I made GY a bracelet and he was really surprised. He is very polite. He even thanked me during appreciations. He never talked during this time. That meant a lot to me. (GY; Day Camp; summer 94)

> We talked about what you can do before you do something. GY is a clown. He likes to make kids laugh. He doesn't think before he does something. We talked about what he could do if someone kept touching him. He said he would turn around and ask them to stop. What is a bad idea if some one kept bugging him? He said I could hit him. Is that a good choice? Why not? I told him he could have really hurt that kid. (GY; One-on-one; 11/9/94)

> GY complimented me on my haircut. "My Mom wanted her hair like that." I said it was like a girl's hair cut on the show "Friends." (GY; One-on-one; 11/7/95)

> CT is a very polite person. I put back a piece and she said, "Do you need this anymore?" She is aware of other's feelings. (CT; One-on-one; 2/21/94)

> HM isn't trying to cheat lately. (HM; One-on-one; 1/31/95)

> She told me she liked my necklace. (MD; One-on-one; 11/21/94)

> Wore her 4-H shirt today and told me thank you. Asked about what the shirt I gave her said. Celebrate 4-H. She didn't know what celebrate meant. I said it meant to be happy, have a party, and tell people what you like about 4-H. She told me all the things she liked. Reading, talking, using markers, using colored pencils, playing games, reading to you, . . . (MD; One-on-one; 4/12/96)

WB is a sweet kid. He knows right from wrong, he knows what is nice and what is rude. He is very respectful. (WB; One-on-one; 5/22/95)

Working on not interrupting people when they talk waiting until finished talking. (RB; One-on-one; 10/12/94)

We played "Go Fish" for the last 10 minutes. She is a good sport. She cheers when others get a match. (RB; One-on-one; 11/14/94)

I see her using her manners a lot more. (RB; One-on-one; 4/5/95)

Very good on social skills. Has fun conversations with me. (RB; One-on-one; 11/3/95)

Gave her a 4-H shirt. She was so excited about it. She thanked me for it. (RB; One-on-one; 4/12/96)

He is doing much better on his loud voice. He talks softer when reminded, usually keeps talking in that tone. We then drew pictures but made him make a story to go along with it. He did fairly well on this. He dictated the sentences and I wrote them for him. (FL; One-on-one; 12/6/93)

As we were working FL said, "I really like your pants." I told him thanks and told him that what he said was very nice. (FL; One-on-one; 2/9/94)

Worked on controlling his temper and listening to directions. (FL; Summer Day camp; 8/14/95)

Enjoyed speaking, giving out compliments, appreciations during camp meetings. (FL; Summer Day camp; 8/14/95)

SW is a nice kid. He got a star performer for excusing himself when he bumped a teacher. (SW; One-on-one; 11/29/95)

We talked about fighting and controlling your anger — because J got suspended for beating this kid up. I said you don't get in trouble because you control your anger. He couldn't tell me what could

Results and Discussion

happen if he doesn't control his anger. He said he likes J but doesn't hang around him because he fights. (SW; One-on-one; 1/17/96)

The above examples help to answer the second research question posed earlier Did the participants' folios exhibit protective factors? From the analysis, 89 examples of specific protective factors of bonding to community, following directions, required helpfulness, and social skills were found in the participants' folios. Five participants each had 10 or more examples of protective factors and the remaining four participants each had 5 to 9 examples of protective factors.

DATA FROM OTHER SOURCES

In reviewing the report cards of the participants, six of the nine participants showed an increase in letter grades. Three participants showed improvement in one subject, one participant showed improvement in two subjects, one participant improved in three subjects, and one participant showed improvement in four subjects. The report cards indicated that five participants showed improvement in reading, three participants showed improvement in math, three participants showed improvement in language, and one participant showed improvement in science.

Three parents completed parent surveys during the time period their child was involved in the program. All three indicated that they felt their child had benefited from participation in the program. Comments from parents included: RB likes school better, has improved their ABC's, the assistant has helped with their child's improvement; LJ is writing better and can spell his name; and FL has more confidence, has improved social skills, is not afraid to talk to people, and knows his numbers.

INDIVIDUAL FOLIOS

In reviewing each participant's individual folio, the following were examined: examples of academic achievement, examples of protective factors, report cards, parent surveys, teacher surveys, and assistant's journal. The comments and statements from the report cards are computer generated. A summary of each participant's folio follows:

RB is a Hispanic female and was in the program from November 1993 to April 1996 while she was in kindergarten through second grade. The assistant observed that RB showed improvement in reading. RB's parent indicated that she had improved in her ABC's, she liked school better, and that she thought the assistant had helped with improvement. Comments from RB's report cards included having difficulty but trying hard, participates and interacts well, and should be commended for effort. RB had 21 examples of academic achievement and 25 examples of protective factors. Two examples follow:

> RB is improving this year. She knows all her letters and most of her sounds. (RB; One-on-one; 5/22/95)

> She seems more confident in herself. (RB; One-on-one; 3/29/96

> WB is a black male and was in the program from January 1994 through April 1996 while he was in kindergarten through second grade. Comments from his report card included: having difficulty but working hard and should be commended for effort. WB had 18 examples of academic achievement and 16 examples of protective factors. Three examples follow:

> He got really excited when I asked him to tell me all the letters he knew on the page. He knew most of them — hard ones were Q and all the vowels. (WB; One-on-one; 2/21/94)

> He started to count his *Skittles* but he got mixed up, if he counted them. I asked, "How can you arrange them so that you know you counted them?" Confused. "Okay, when you were in kindergarten last year how did you move your counters to . . . ?" Didn't have to finish — he started to align them in a row and counted. Did a wonderful job. (WB; One-on-one; 3/29/95)

> At 4-H, F came in for her class. I told F that I could help her after 4-H. WB said he would like to help too. We all helped F move chairs into the gym. WB is a very giving person. (WB; One-on-one; 3/25/96)

LJ is a black male and was in the program from November 1993 through April 1996 while he was in kindergarten through second grade. The assistant noted that he had built higher order thinking skills, he had improved a great deal in his social skills, and he had improved in reading and self-confidence. LJ's parent stated that his

Results and Discussion

writing was better and that he could spell his name. Comments from LJ's report cards included: needs to make better use of time, should be commended for effort, and consistently tries hard. LJ had 25 examples of academic achievement and 26 examples of protective factors. Three examples follow:

> Wow. I had to make sure this was LJ. He was non-stop talk. He was telling me about his Mom & Dad, what he got for Christmas, that he can't play in the snow, . . . I was so surprised. It was really nice. He even smiled when I praised him for knowing all his colors. (LJ; One-on-one; 1/10/94)

> It is hard to believe that this is the same kid I worked with in kindergarten. He smiles, shows his feelings, he hugs me, talks, shares what he thinks, and he "fights" for what he thinks is right. When I worked with LJ in kindergarten, he was not self-confident, didn't try, didn't smile, and was very hard to talk to. (LJ; One-on-one; 4/12/95)

> Said he wanted to read to me. He went down to get two stories for him to read. He read wonderfully! He has come a long way. Still very hard on himself. Had a big smile when I clapped. (LJ; One-on-one; 3/8/96)

CT is a black female who was in the program from November 1993 to March 1996 while she was in the first through third grades. The assistant noted that CT had more self-confidence and she had good thinking and problem solving skills. CT's report cards showed improvement in reading and math. Comments from CT's report card included: reads own and class generated writing, completes homework consistently, consistently tries hard, showing improvement, and needs encouragement. CT had 47 examples of academic achievement and 42 examples of protective factors. Two examples follow:

> We worked on three pages on phonics. She has come a long way. When I first introduced her she could tell me all the sounds of the alphabet, now she can read the words knowing most of the words. (CT; One-on-one; 4/20/94)

CT talks more than she did last year. I think she feels more comfortable with me — I am a familiar face. Still is quiet though. (CT; One-on-one; 10/24/94)

FL is a black male and was in the program from November 1993 to March 1996 while he was in the first through third grades. The assistant observed that he read better and his math had improved. FL's report card showed improvement in reading. Comments from his report card included: having difficulty but working hard, should be commended for effort, consistently tries hard, showing improvement, needs encouragement, comes to class prepared to work, and has positive attitude toward math. FL had 21 examples of academic achievement and 45 examples of protective factors. Two examples follow:

FL comes to visit me every morning I am here. He gives me a hug and shares something about himself (shirt, weekend, Mom, Dad.) He loves to talk. He is a helper at lunch and is doing a good job. (FL; One-on-one; 11/2/94)

Hooray! FL read his sentences, using his fingers to follow along. He didn't start making up his own sentence. I started off telling him what I expected from him and he did really well. (FL; One-on-one; 12/12/94)

MD is a white female and was in the program from September 1994 to April 1996 while she was in the first and second grades. MD's report card revealed improvement in reading, language, and math. Comments from her report card included: consistently tries hard, needs to listen and follow directions, and should be commended for effort. MD had 17 examples of academic achievement and 19 examples of protective factors. Two examples follow:

Did a super job matching beginning sound with pictures. She had no trouble at all. Worked well by herself too. She did really well at matching upper to lower case letters. (MD; One-on-one; 11/30/94)

Came up to me in the cafeteria at breakfast and hugged me. Asked about me picking her up. (MD; One-on-one; 2/1/96)

SW is a black male and was in the program from November 1992 to March 1996 while he was in the second through fifth grades. The assistant reported that his art teacher told the assistant that she could see great improvement in SW's self-esteem. SW's report card showed improvement in reading, math, language, and science. Comments from his report card included: puts forth great effort, has pride in developing literacy, has positive attitude toward math, courteous dependable worker, shows good effort, shows interest in books, uses logical reasoning, works well with others, and showing improvement, and needs encouragement. SW had 11 examples of academic achievement and 33 examples of protective factors. Four examples follow:

> Word cards and math review. SW's attitude has improved so much; his confidence is building more and more. He is working with Mrs. B. She is his math/reading lab teacher. Our materials are consistent with hers in order to keep SW focused. I'm so proud of him. He says that he's studying his cards at home before he's allowed to play. He says he's doing this almost everyday. (SW; One-on-one; 11/9/92)

> SW is doing so well, his attitude is so much better. He's opening up more. I could see the progress in his journal. He's forming complete sentences now and has improved in his spelling, I'm so happy for him. (SW; One-on-one; 11/23/93)

> Mrs. G stopped me in the hall and told me the teachers were talking about how happy SW is this year. She said it is all my doing. I said I think his confidence level is high because he sees success in the self-contained classroom. (SW; One-on-one; 3/7/95)

> With SW, I see that being there for him 2 years in a row, has helped him come out and share things I would never dream. I learned in a meeting that kids learn and care more if you care and have enthusiasm. (SW; One-on-one; 3/28/95)

HM is a white male who was in the program from November 1993 to November 1995 while he was in the third through the fifth grade. The assistant noted that his relationship with the assistant steadily improved over the time he was involved with the program, as did his social and problem solving skills. A comment from his report card was having difficulty but working hard. HM had three examples of academic achievement and 17 examples of protective factors. One example follows:

> Always stops in to talk to me before school. (HM; One-on-one; 1/31/95)

GY is a white male and was in the program from June 1994 to March 1996 while he was in the second and third grades. GY's report card showed improvement in language. Comments from his report card included: participates and interacts well, demonstrates good self-discipline, shows good effort, and showing improvement. GY had 22 examples of academic achievement and 41 examples of protective factors. Two examples follow:

> GY's behavior is very different when he is with me. Listens, doesn't talk back — knows and follows rules. (GY; One-on-one; 10/24/94)

> We worked on word find/finish the sentence. GY said it was easy. We did another activity where he found a word using the first letter from each picture. GY is a good speller. (GY; One-on-one; 11/9/94)

RESEARCH QUESTIONS

The research questions for this investigation were:

I. Did the participants' folios exhibit evidence of protective factors?
II. Did the participants exhibit an increase in academic achievement?

The data collected were both qualitative (one-on-one observation forms, journals, and teacher and parent surveys) and quantitative (report cards). The data provided rich sources of evidence of protective factors and academic achievement for the individual participants. This method of gathering data, while time consuming for the program assistant, proved valuable in determining if protective factors were found and if academic achievement did occur for the individual participants in the program. In reporting the data, the authors have provided results both in a qualitative, narrative form and in a numerical, quantitative form. Generalizations should be made with

Results and Discussion

caution because of the qualitative nature of this case study. Frequency data is provided to reveal trends. However number and variety of data vary in each folio.

In reviewing the data, 264 examples of protective factors were found in the participants' folios. Three participants each had over 40 examples of protective factors, one participant had between 31 and 40 examples of protective factors, two participants each had between 21 and 30 examples of protective factors, and three participants each had between 16 and 20 examples of protective factors. The protective factors ranged from:

- likes of the participant (54 examples),
- relationship with adults (33 examples),
- social skills (32 examples),
- positive behavior (29 examples),
- self-concept (26 examples),
- family (24 examples),
- following directions, (23 examples),
- bonding to community (18 examples),
- required helpfulness (16 examples) and
- relationships with peers (9 examples).

When considering the eight protective factors that were used in the original design of the Model City/Woodland Wilkie Literacy Project, evidence was found that those protective factors did occur:

- positive school experience (185 examples of academic achievement),
- adult relationships (33 examples),
- social skills (32 examples),
- self-esteem (26 examples),
- bonding to community (18 examples),
- required helpfulness (16 examples),
- problem solving (7 examples), and
- close friend (7 examples).

All five levels of protective factors — individual (social skills, self-esteem, and problem solving); family (adult relationships); peer (close friend); school (positive school experience); and community (bonding to community and required helpfulness) were affected. The program focused on youth participants but in reality affected other concentric circles of family, school, peers, and community as described in Bronfennbrenner's ecological framework.

Examples of increased academic achievement were found 185 times in the participants' folios. Five of the participants each had over 20 examples of increased academic achievement, two participants each had between 15 and 20 examples, one participant had 11 examples, and one participant had 3 examples.

Table 4 and Table 5 provide the ordered rankings of the participants' examples of protective factors and academic achievement. When the participants were ranked in order from the most examples of protective factors to the least number of examples of protective factors, the following was found:

Two of the three participants who had the most academic achievement examples, also exhibited the second and third highest ranking of examples of protective factors.

The two participants who had the seventh and ninth ranking of academic achievement examples, also exhibited the seventh and eighth ranking of protective factors.

Table 4: Participants Ranked by Number of Protective Factor Examples

Participant	Protective Factor Examples	Academic Achievement Examples
FL	45	21
CT	42	47
GY	41	22
SW	33	11
LJ	26	25
RB	25	21
MD	19	17
HM	17	3
WB	16	18

Results and Discussion

Table 5: Participants Ranked by Number of Academic Achievement Examples

Participant	Academic Achievement Examples	Protective Factor Examples
CT	47	42
LJ	25	26
GY	22	41
FL	21	45
RB	21	25
WB	18	16
MD	17	19
SW	11	33
HM	3	17

When comparing the number of protective factors to academic achievement examples for each participant, 5 of 9 appear to be nearly equally balanced, but 2 have twice as many protective factors as academic achievement examples, and 2 have very limited academic achievement examples in proportion to protective factors. This finding is consistent with Wallerstein and Kelly's (1980) conclusion that resilient children (those with higher levels of protective factors) were apt to do well in school (increased academic achievement.)

When the participants were grouped into grade levels of when they participated in the program of K-2nd (3 participants), 1st-3rd (3 participants), and 2nd-5th (3 participants), the data revealed that:

- K-2nd participants had an average of 21 examples of academic achievement and 22 examples of protective factors,
- 1st-3rd participants had an average of 25 examples of academic achievement and 35 examples of protective factors, and
- 2nd-5th participants had an average of 12 examples of academic achievement and 30 examples of protective factors.

The 1st-3rd participants had the most examples of both academic achievement and protective factors. For this sample of participants, the most progress was found with the 1st-3rd participants.

In looking at those same grade levels, the 2nd-5th participants had most examples in problem solving, positive behavior, likes, bonding to community, problem behavior, required helpfulness, and social skills. The K-2nd participants had the most examples of increased math skills and self-concept. The 1st-3rd participants had the most examples of increased reading skills, increased spelling skills, increased science skills, increased language skills, family, adult relationships, relationships with peers, and following directions.

In reviewing the quantitative data from the report cards of the participants, only six of the nine participants showed an increase in academic achievement, by improving at least one letter grade in a subject. The three who did not show any improvement were all males. Two of the participants (LJ and WB) were in grades K-2 and one (HM) was in grades 2-5. The folios of the three participants who did not show an increase in letter grades indicated the following:

HM's folio showed the lowest number of examples of academic achievement (3 examples) and the second lowest number of examples of protective factors (17 examples). His letter grades stayed the same. He was referred to the Literacy Project for classroom behavior problems and continued to struggle with these problems.

LJ's folio revealed that his academic level was very low when he began in the Literacy Project. His letter grades stayed the same. Both of his parents displayed poor parenting skills (shoplifting and drug use).

WB's folio showed that his academic level was very low when he began the Literacy Project. WB had the fewest number of examples of protective factors (16 examples). His letter grades stayed the same. There was a lack of family involvement/interest shown by his parents.

Three participants showed improvement in one subject, one participant showed improvement in two subjects, one participant showed improvement in three subjects, and one participant showed improvement in four subjects. The report cards indicated that:

- five participants showed improvement in reading,
- three participants showed improvement in math,
- three participants showed improvement in language, and
- one participant showed improvement in science.

When the participants were grouped into grade levels of when they participated in the program of K-2nd, 1st-3rd, and 2nd-5th, the data revealed that the K-2nd participants had improved in only one subject, the 1st-3rd participants had improved in 6 subjects, and the 2nd-5th participants had improved in 5 subjects. Consistent with the folio data, the report card findings indicate the most progress was

Results and Discussion

found with the 1st-3rd grade participants. The combination of the data from the one-on-one observation forms and the report cards indicate that the participants exhibited an increase in academic achievement.

A major focus of the Model City/Woodland Wilkie Literacy Project was literacy and increased reading skills. Reading is a basic skill needed for all students as they progress in elementary school and beyond. The data revealed that five of the nine participants' report cards showed improvement in reading, each of the nine participants' folios included examples of increased reading skills, and that six of the nine participants had more examples of increased reading skills than any other area of academic achievement.

CHAPTER V
Implications

This chapter deals with the practical significance of the present results. The first section deals with suggestions for the staff of Model City/Woodland Wilkie Literacy Project to make changes in programming efforts and the second section makes recommendations for youth programming. The third section suggests a future research agenda.

RECOMMENDATIONS FOR THE MODEL CITY/WOODLAND WILKIE LITERACY PROJECT

Continue to focus on the importance of the positive relationship with a caring adult. Progress was made in building a strong relationship between the assistant and the participants. The assistant served as a building block of the microsystem between the participant and the school. Additional work needs to be done on helping the participants build relationships with other caring adults in the community.

The data collection procedures need to be more deliberate and intentional from the very beginning of the Literacy Project. More time needs to be built into the assistants' days, especially during summer day camp, to help ensure that the data collection is occurring at all sites and by all assistants.

Hire staff who are committed to and understand the importance of data collection.

Continue to intentionally design programs that help to increase protective factors in young people in all levels of their life — individual, family, peer, school, and community.

Implications

Valuable data regarding students' protective factors and academic achievement can be gathered by the use of observation forms by the one-on-one tutor. Continue this method of gathering data.

RECOMMENDATIONS FOR YOUTH PROGRAMMING

Encourage collection of qualitative data by volunteers and staff as they work with young people in their programs, especially those youth who they may potentially work with for many years. This method of gathering data would be useful in other aspects of youth programming such as 4-H community clubs, after school groups, and special interest clubs. Consider using journaling as a method of gathering data. The dilemma is the time intensity it takes for a staff member or volunteer to devote to the concentrated recording of observations.

Intentionally design programs which help to increase protective factors in young people in all levels of their life — individual, family, peer, school, and community.

Facilitate ways for youth professionals and volunteers need to focus on providing young people the opportunity to bond with a supportive adult in their programming efforts.

FUTURE RESEARCH AGENDA

Gather data on the cost effectiveness of having additional staff at elementary schools who can be devoted to a small number of students to focus on building protective factors and increasing academic achievement. Does the cost of hiring such staff pay off in the long run? Do the students stay in school? Do their grades improve? Do they shy away from risky behavior?

Conduct a follow-up study on these nine participants when they reach middle school to see if they continue to exhibit protective factors and maintain the progress of their academic achievement.

APPENDIX A
One-On-One Evaluation Form

One-on-One
Evaluation Form
School Year

Child's Name _____ Afternoon Kindergarten   Date 11-22-93
1st day

This week, how do you feel about school?
In general?

What do you like best?

Notes:
Behavior/Discipline:
very quiet
It seems as if he doesn't enjoy much.

Self Concept (Look for words like, I can/can't, gestures, eye contact):
doesn't smile
No eye contact

Tutoring:
Reading: Mrs. Pocek gave me a list of things for _____ to work on.
Colors: 8 basic, pink, gray
Shapes
Counting to 20
Sequencing
Math: opposites
Copying
Spatial relationships - behind, between
writing name.
Science:

Comments:
Today we worked on writing name, copying, shapes, + colors.

He knows blue + black the rest he guesses
Shapes - knows circle and square but oval, rectangle + triangle is hard for him.

Copying - he is working on holding his pencil correctly
He held it like a fist. He needs to work on fine motor skills.

APPENDIX B
Parent Survey

PHONE/HOME VISIT SURVEY: PARTICIPANT PROGRESS
MODEL CITY WOODLAND WILLKIE LITERACY PROJECT
AUGUST, 1994

Hi, this is (your name), from ISU Extension, Polk County. Your (son, daughter, name) was in the 4-H program at (school name) during the last year with (Alyson, Chet, Filice, Kevin, or Leeann.) We're doing year-end evaluation, and I'd like to ask you a few questions if that's ok with you. (If they say it's ok, go on. If not, thank them and note on the list.)

1. Do you think (child's name) has gained self confidence through 4-H?

   ___✓___ yes _____ no   (If yes,) What are some things you've noticed?
   writing is better, can spell his
   name

2. Has (child's name) improved their school work this year? (examples: better grades, attitude)

   ___✓___ yes _____ no   (If yes), What improvements have you seen?
   _____
   _____

3. What do you think has caused the improvements? (examples: luck, hard work, better teacher, 4-H)
   Combination of things

4. What does (child's name) think has caused the improvements?
   hard work

5. Do you think (child's name) has developed friendships through 4-H?

   ___✓___ yes _____ no

6. How often did you go to school event last year?   Number _can't remember_

7. Was that more, less or the same number as in the past?

   _____ more _____ less ___✓___ the same

8. Are anything else you'd like to say about the program or about your family? (write notes on back, etc.) _no_

APPENDIX C
Teacher Survey

IOWA STATE UNIVERSITY
OF SCIENCE AND TECHNOLOGY
Cooperative Extension

1-1 M&W
2:00-2:15

Polk County Center
[address illegible]
Des Moines, Iowa [zip]
[phone]
FAX [number]
Email polk@exnet.iastate.edu

SURVEY QUESTIONS

Kindergarten

1. Does student exhibit responsible behavior in the classroom?
   uses appropriate behavior, respects authority, sometimes/frequently is [illegible] to get him [illegible] - he [illegible], etc.

2. Does student have a positive attitude towards learning?
   He works and gets it done. He is not enthusiastic nor does he "complain" about work being [done/hard].

3. Does student interact well in the classroom?
   He does not speak in group situations. In smaller group of 2-3 he opens up more.

   Academic Record — sight vocabulary low
   Reading — does not "hear" beginning sounds
   Language — below — works w/ speech teacher
   Spelling
   Handwriting — needs to be in control of pencils
   Math — does know 1, 2 objects (far as we [gone]) counts to 13
   Science/Health — below grade level
   Art
   Music
   P.E.
   Social Studies

APPENDIX D
Journal Entry

I am trying to ask questions that he can't answer w/ yes or no or fine. He opened up today. He really spent time talking today. I met his father today. He said "He always picks me up and drops me off. My mom doesn't do anything." I thought it was funny when he said it but asked if she works. She does work so probably has a hard time doing the "school thing."

One thing that makes me sad w/ _____ is that I never see feelings from him. He doesn't smile, doesn't get angry. He just does what he has to. I even saw him out for recess and he wasn't smiling. He looked w/ no feeling.

We worked on patterning today. He did really well at making the pattern after he saw it. He did really well at his name. He wrote it in between the lines. He didn't have all the letters but he showed me he could hold his pencil correctly & strong.

We were working w/ chips today. They stack up well, he started making a tower with them. I think if he had more fine motor skills activities, this would improve his writing skills. We had fun making the tower.

References

Adams, G., Adams-Taylor, S., & Pittman, K. (1989). Adolescent pregnancy and parenthood: A review of the problem, solutions, and resources. *Family Relations, 38,* 223-229.

Anthony, E. J. (1974). Introduction: The syndrome of the psychologically invulnerable child. In E. J. Anthony & C. Koupernik (Eds.), *The child in his family: Vol. 3. Children at psychiatric risk* (pp. 3-10). New York: Wiley.

Antonovsky, A. (1979). *Health, stress and coping: New perspectives on mental and physical well-being.* San Francisco: Jossey-Bass.

Benard, B. (1987). Protective factor research: What we can learn from resilient children. *Illinois Prevention Forum. 7,* 3-10.

Benard, B. (1991, August). *Fostering resiliency in kids: Protective factors in the family, school, and community.* Oakbrook, IL: Midwest Regional Center for Drug-Free Schools and Communities.

Benson, P. L. (1990). *The troubled journey: A portrait of 6th-12th grade youth.* Minneapolis, MN: Lutheran Brotherhood.

Berlin, G. & Sum, A. (1988). *Toward a more perfect union: Basic skills, poor families, and our economic future.* New York: Ford Foundation.

Bleuler, M. (1984). Different forms of childhood stress and patterns of adult psychiatric outcome. In N. Watt, E. J. Anthony, L. Wynne, & J. Rolf, (Eds.), *Children at-risk for schizophrenia: A longitudinal perspective.* (pp. 537-542). New York: Cambridge University Press.

Block, J. (1981). Growing up vulnerable and growing up resistant: Two longitudinal studies: Preschool personality, preadolescent personality, and intervening family stresses. In C.D. Moore (Ed.), *Adolescence and stress.* (pp. 123-147). Washington, D.C.: U.S. Government Printing Office.

References

Bogenschneider, K. (1996). Family related prevention programs: An ecological risk/protective theory for building prevention programs, policies, and community capacity to support youth. *Family Relations, 45,* 127-138.

Bogenschneider, K. (1997). Parental involvement in adolescent schooling: A proximal process with transcontextual validity. *Journal of Marriage and the Family, 59,* 718-733.

Borg, W. R. & Gall, M D. (1989). *Educational Research.* New York: Longman.

Brendtro, L. K., Brokenleg, M., & Van Bockern, S. (1990). *Reclaiming youth at risk: Our hope for the future.* Bloomington, IL: National Education Service.

Bronfenbrenner, U. (1979). *The ecology of human development: Experiments by nature and design.* Boston: Harvard University Press.

Bronfenbrenner, U. (1986a). Ecology of the family as a context for human development: Research perspectives. *Developmental Psychology, 22*(6), 723-742.

Bronfenbrenner, U. (1986b). Recent advances in research on the ecology of human development. In R. K. Silbereisen, K. Eyferth, & G. Rudinger (Eds.), *Development as action in context: Problem behavior and normal youth development* (pp. 287-309). Heidlberg and New York: Springer-Verlag.

Carnegie Council on Adolescent Development (1996). *Great transitions: Preparing adolescents for a new century.* New York: Carnegie Corporation of New York.

Carnegie Council on Adolescent Development (1989). *Turning points: Preparing American youth for the 21st century.* New York: Carnegie Corporation of New York.

Children's Defense Fund (1996). *The state of America's children yearbook 1996.* Washington, DC: Children's Defense Fund.

Clark, R. M. (1983). *Family life and school achievement: Why poor black children succeed or fail.* Chicago: University of Chicago Press.

Des Moines Public School District. (1995, July). *Report of school suspensions 1994-95* (No. PAS577.1). Des Moines, IA: Des Moines Public School District.

Dryfoos, J. G. (1990). *Adolescents at risk: Prevalence and prevention.* New York: Oxford University Press.

Edelman, M. W. (1987). *Families in peril: An agenda for social change.* Cambridge, MA.: Harvard University Press.

Elder, G. H., Jr. (1974). *Children of the great depression.* Chicago: University of Chicago Press.

Epstein, J. L. (1983). Longitudinal effects of family-school-person interactions on student outcomes. *Research in Sociology of Education and Socialization, 4,* 101-127.

Garbarino, J. (1992). *Children and families in the social environment* (2nd ed.). New York: Aldine Publishing Company.

Garbarino, J. (1984). *The evolution of an ecological perspective on human development.* Opening session of the Research Workshop, Education and Support for Parenting: An Ecological Perspective on Primary Prevention. University of Victoria, Victoria, Canada.

Garmezy, N. (1985). Stress resistant children: The search for protective factors. In J. E. Stevenson (Ed.), *Aspects of current child psychiatry research, Journal of child psychology and psychiatry, Book Supplement 4.* (pp. 213-233). Oxford, England: Pergamon.

Garmezy, N. & Rutter, M. (Eds.). (1983). *Stress, coping and development in children.* New York: McGraw-Hill.

Gibbs, J. & Bennett, S. (1990). *Together we care: A framework for community prevention planning.* Seattle: Comprehensive Health Education Foundation.

Hawkins, J. D., Catalano, R. F., & Miller, J. F. (1992). Risk and protective factors for alcohol and other drug problems in adolescence and early adulthood: Implications for substance abuse prevention. *Psychological Bulletin, 112,* 64-105.

Hawkins, J. D., Lishner, D. M., Catalano, R. F., & Howard, M. O. (1985). Childhood predictors of adolescent substance abuse. *Journal of Children in Contemporary Society, 18* (1-2), 11-48.

Higgins, P. & Mueller, D. (1988). *The prevention of poor school performance and school failure: A literature review.* St. Paul, MN: Amherst H. Wilder Foundation.

Iowa Kids Count (1995). *Baselines and benchmarks: Indicators of well-being for Iowa Children.* Des Moines, IA: Iowa Kids Count.

Leffert, N., Benson, P. L., & Roehlkepartain, J. L. (1997). *Starting out right: Developmental assets for children.* Minneapolis, MN: Search Institute.

Lofquist, W. A. & Miller, M. G. (1989). *Inventory of adult attitudes and behavior: An instrument for examining the nature of adult/youth relationships.* Tucson, AZ: Associates for Youth Development Publications.

Masten, A. S., Best, K. M., & Garmezy, N. (1990). Resilience and development: Contributions from the study of children who overcome adversity. *Development and Psychopathology, 2,* 425-444.

References

McKnight, J. L. (1993). A sampling of ideas for involving schools in community revitalization. *Equity and Choice, 9,* 30-31.

Moskovitz, S. (1983). *Love despite hate: Child survivors of the holocaust and their adult lives.* New York: Schocken.

Murphy, L. & Moriarty, A. (1976). *Vulnerability, coping and growth from infancy to adolescence.* New Haven, CT: Yale University Press.

National Commission of Children (U.S.) (1991). *Beyond rhetoric: A new American agenda for children and families.* Washington, DC: National Commission on Children.

Newman, B. & Newman, P. (1986). *Adolescent development.* Columbus, OH: Merrill Publishing.

Pines, M.(1984). PT conversation: Michael Rutter: Resilient children, *Psychology Today, 18,* 60,62,64-65.

Pittman, K. J. (1990, October). *Challenges to the profession: A call to action to those in youth services.* Keynote address to the 1990 Youth Leadership Symposium, University of Northern Iowa, Cedar Falls, IA.

Rutter, M. (1978). Early sources of security and competence. In J. Brunner & A. Garton. (Eds.), *Human growth and development.*(pp. 33-61). New York: Oxford University Press.

Rutter, M. (1985). Resilience in the face of adversity: Protective factors and resistance to psychiatric disorder. *British Journal of Psychiatry, 147,* 598-611.

Rutter, M. (1987). Psychosocial resilience and protective mechanisms. *American Journal of Orthopsychiatry, 57,* 316-331.

Rutter, M.; Maughan, B.; Mortimore, P.; & Ousten, J. with Smith, A. (1979). *Fifteen thousand hours: Secondary schools and their effect on children.* Cambridge, MA: Harvard University Press.

Schorr, L. B. (1988) *Within our reach.* New York: Doubleday.

Slavin, R., Karweit, N., & Wasik, B. (Eds.). (1994) *Preventing early school failure.* Boston: Allyn and Bacon.

Small, S. A. & Eastman, G. (1991). Rearing adolescents in contemporary society: A conceptual framework for understanding the responsibilities and needs of parents. *Family Relations, 40,* 455-462.

Small, S., Silverberg, S., & Kerns, D. (1992). Adolescents' perceptions of the cost and benefits of engaging in health-compromising behaviors. *Journal of Youth and Adolescence, 22,* 73-87.

Steinberg, L. (1986). Latchkey children and susceptibility to peer pressure: An ecological approach. *Developmental Psychology, 22,* 433-439.

Steinberg, L. (1989). *Adolescent transitions and substance abuse prevention*. Monograph commissioned and distributed by the U.S. Office of Substance Abuse Prevention, Washington, D.C.

Turner, S. & Handler M. (1991). Data Collector [Computer software]. Santa Barbara, CA: Intellimation.

Wallerstein, J. S. & Kelly, J. B. (1980). *Surviving the breakup: How children and parents cope with divorce*. New York: Basic Books.

Werner, E. E. (1989a, April). Children of the garden island. *Scientific American, 206,* 106-111.

Werner, E. E. (1989b). High risk children in young adulthood: A longitudinal study from birth to 32 years. *American Journal of Orthopsychiatry, 59*(1), 72-81.

Werner, E. E. (1990). Protective factors and individual resilience. In S.J. Meisels & J. P. Shonkoff (Eds.) *Handbook of early childhood intervention* (pp. 97-116). Cambridge, England: Cambridge University Press.

Werner, E. E. & Smith, R.S. (1982). *Vulnerable but invincible: A longitudinal study of resilient children and youth*. New York: McGraw-Hill.

Yin, R. K. (1984). *Case study research: Design and methods*. Beverly Hills, CA: Sage Publications.

Index

Achievement motivation, 19
Bonding to social institutions, 28, 69
Close friend, 23, 60
Close relationship with adult, 21, 32, 60
Ecological model of human development, 9
Exosystem, 11
Extra curricular activities, 25
Faith community, 19
Family support, 21, 58
Hobbies, 18
Macrosystem, 11
Mesosystem, 10
Microsystem, 10
Parental monitoring, 22
Positive school experience, 24, 32
Problem solving skills, 17, 57
Protective factors, 7, 12, 14, 17, 30, 80, 81, 82, 86, 87
Required helpfulness, 26, 32, 71
Risk factors, 7, 13, 14
Self-esteem, 18
Supportive community, 27

For Product Safety Concerns and Information please contact our EU representative GPSR@taylorandfrancis.com
Taylor & Francis Verlag GmbH, Kaufingerstraße 24, 80331 München, Germany

www.ingramcontent.com/pod-product-compliance
Lightning Source LLC
Chambersburg PA
CBHW051103230426
43667CB00013B/2429